THE HUMAN CHURCH

THE HUMAN CHURCH

William H. DuBay

1966

DOUBLEDAY & COMPANY, INC.

GARDEN CITY, NEW YORK

Grateful acknowledgment is made to the following for permission to reprint the following material.

THE AMERICA PRESS – From *Mater et Magistra, Christianity and Social Progress* by Pope John XXIII.

BEACON PRESS – From *Black Religion, The Negro and Christianity in the United States* by Joseph R. Washington, Jr. Copyright © 1964 by Joseph R. Washington, Jr.

BLAISDELL PUBLISHING COMPANY, a division of Ginn and Company – From *Constitutional Government and Democracy* by Carl J. Friedrich.

CHICAGO STUDIES – From "Democratic Structures in the Church" from *Chicago Studies.*

DOUBLEDAY & COMPANY, INC. – From *The Book of the Acts of God* by G. Ernest Wright and Reginald H. Fuller.

DUQUESNE UNIVERSITY PRESS – From *Truth and Freedom* by Louis de Raeymaeker, *et al.*

HOLT, RINEHART AND WINSTON, INC. – From *My People Is the Enemy* by William Stringfellow.

HOUGHTON MIFFLIN COMPANY – From *Government in Modern Society* by R. Wallace Brewster.

THE RELIGIOUS EDUCATION ASSOCIATION of the United States and Canada – From "Prejudice Reduction in Religious Education" by Henry Cohen, published originally in *Religious Education,* September–October, 1964, New York City.

Quotations from Scripture are from *The Holy Bible,* the Confraternity of Christian Doctrine edition, except for the quotation from I SAMUEL on page 109, which is from *The Complete Bible* (University of Chicago Press), and the quotation from MATTHEW 22 on page 157, which is from *The New English Bible* (Oxford University Press).

FIRST EDITION

Library of Congress Catalog Card Number 65–23792

Printed in the United States of America

In honor of the memory of
JOHN XXIII
a pope who led

INTRODUCTION

The difference between the Angry Young Men and the Angry Old Men is that the Old Men have more to lose and the Young Men have less to work with. This means that the Young Men have to choose their targets carefully, aim with precision, and not waste ammunition. Not that they have any bloodshed in mind, but they must speak forcibly and to the point.

The remarkable thing about the church is that the conversation is actually taking place. People are being honest with one another about what they deeply feel. There is honesty in the church after all. It is important that the Young Men and the Old Men stay angry and that a lot of others become angry and express what they feel too. The only thing we have to fear is that they keep their feelings to themselves. It is in the hope of breaking a little ice that the author offers this work.

I wish to thank the comrades-in-arms throughout the world whose inspiration, suggestions, and support have contributed to this book in so many ways.

William H. DuBay
Chaplain, Saint John's Hospital
Santa Monica, California

CONTENTS

THE HUMAN CHURCH

CHAPTER ONE

God for Us

The greatest contribution of the Hebrew people to religion was that they did away with it. Their great mission has been to tell the rest of the world that religion is just not a legitimate occupation for man. In the school of cruel experience they have learned that religious ambition is a vain and dangerous pursuit indeed. They have found out that the knowledge of God is not only impossible but inhuman.

The Hebrews did not come to this insight as a result of philosophical development but by historical experience. They did not pursue Yahweh, but were pursued by him. They did not please him with the works of religion. Rather it was his pleasure to use them to destroy the works of religion. He was the god-slayer who set out to vanquish not only the deities of the world but also man's pretense to do business with God. Yahweh was the first atheist, the great iconoclast and demythologizer. He showed up religious systems for what they often were: the real oppressors and tyrants of men. He was intolerant of mystical rites and arcane knowledge which men used to terrorize others. Religion was an abomination to him, not only because it was used for purposes of social control, but because it placed God outside the secular world in which man lives. The Hebrews found out that God is met not in some mystical or cultic experience, but in service of the secular.

The first concept they had of God was his absolute unapproachability. Man can never attain God or know him. God is absolute and independent. Man is terribly contingent and fiercely dependent on his own environs. Salvation for man does not consist in speculation about the inscrutable, unknowable, and absolute nature of God, but in the development of man's happiness. If God chooses to reveal himself to man, it can only be in terms of man's contingent needs and subjective drive for happiness. When God speaks to man, it is not about God but about man. "For my thoughts are not your thoughts, nor are your ways my ways, says the LORD. As high as the heavens are above the earth, so high are my ways above your ways and my thoughts above your thoughts." (ISAIAH 55:8–9.)

The second concept they had of God was the nearness of his word. They could never attain the commander, but his command was always close at hand. Since this command had to do with their own human and earthly happiness, it was radically and thoroughly secular. The history of the Hebrews demonstrates that God's command is found in all the circumstances and situations of human life. If man is to be saved, he has only to recognize that command and obey it. Salvation is not something to be plucked from the skies, wrested from the tomes of philosophy, or manipulated by religious rites, but is found in the service of the secular. God revealed himself in the history of the Hebrews not to remove man from the world, but to show him how to find salvation within it. The world does not need God; God is already in it. What the world does need is man—man fully arrived at his capacity to be, not divine, but human.

Religion seems to thrive on two grand delusions. The first is the hostility of the gods, who must be appeased. Everybody at times has a fear of the unknown. Death, suffering, the unpredictable misfortunes of life, and rampant injustice are big question marks for mankind. There must be some reason for them. We attribute to the gods the final explanation. If they are not actually hostile to us, we feel they should at least be able to control some of the tragedies that befall us. This has always been the purpose of religion: to provide men with some means of coping with their fears of the unknown. If we can get to the gods, they can make things better for us. With the right combination of mystical ceremonies and sacrificial gifts offered inside the proper temples, we might someday please the gods. And then we will have it made.

The other delusion is the conviction of man's natural goodness to man. Religion has always been used as a tool to convince people that they are very good to one another, no matter how strong the evidence to the contrary. If you are down in the dumps, out of work, tired of being a slave or fighting wars, don't blame other people; they really have your best interests at heart, even though you may not understand them. Instead let us gather in our places of worship to pat one another on the back and to congratulate ourselves on how kind we are. If only the gods were as understanding and humane as we are, then our troubles would be over. Religion never has much effect on them, but it certainly is worth the expense for ourselves. No matter how guilty and insecure we are, we can go to church and have all our doubts smothered in the sweet sauce of praise: praise for the wisdom of our forebears, praise for the accomplishments of our leaders, praise for the appropriateness of our worship, and praise, in short, for ourselves. No matter how great the world's problems, they can all be solved so simply by more of what we have right here: good will, mutual solicitude, and efficiency—all wrapped up in the decor of good taste and propriety.

The god of the Hebrews made his appearance to do away with this nonsense. He has no use for churches, is in the habit of knocking them down as a matter of fact. Exercises of religion are an insult to him; he is incensed by incense and mortified by mortification. What need does he have for ceremonies and sacrifices? And what need does man have for them? Is not Yahweh good enough for him? What can man gain from the practices of religion that Yahweh has not already given him? Yahweh is already on man's side, much more than man is. He is not the kind of a god that sits around waiting to be prodded into action by the invocations of pious assemblies. He is not going to be finagled into anything and lets it be known that he is in full control of himself. The one who brought the whole world into play is not himself going to be brought into play by some secret rites. He knows what he is about and is quite sure of himself in his role. He refuses to be tied down to any office hours corresponding to the parish program of worship; he is much too busy managing the destinies of people and nations. He is not going to stop the world and listen to the incantations and advice of people who think he should. He is not going to be blamed, finally, for man's troubles. The Hebrews have learned better than to go to Yahweh for relief; he only shows them where the real problems are.

The Hebrews have also learned about man's humanity to man. Man is not exactly a social animal, and the Hebrews have the scars to prove it. Throughout their history they have had their problems and are quite familiar with the tyranny of brotherhood. The Hebrews have been sold into slavery, exiled, crucified, betrayed, bombed, gassed, and exterminated. Perhaps better than the rest of us, they know that man is a competitive, aggressive, dominating, and exploiting individual. With a brother like that, one doesn't need any enemies. And this is just what the history and literature of the Hebrews have to tell us: we've got the whole thing backwards. God is not against us; we are against us. Man has no need to pacify his gods, but his brother. Man has no need for God; he already has him. He has need for his brother; he has lost him. What Yahweh told the Hebrews and the rest of us is that our problems are basically human problems, not problems for the gods. God answers our needs by enabling us to answer them. People need people.

We all suspect that God has not really played his trump;

he's withholding something that would give us the key to everything. It's a messed-up world and God's fault for our not being able to figure it out. But Yahweh's cards are on the table for all of us to see. This world we are in is all he has to show. If it is not an ideal one, don't blame him. He has given us all the instructions for running it; if it fails to function properly, the manufacturer will not assume the responsibility. Man's problems are not that the world is badly put together but that he himself is made so well: free and self-determining. It's not that the gods do not appreciate man's needs, but that man does not appreciate his own capacity. It's not that God is inhuman, but man is.

There is just no alternative to this world; we just have to learn to live in it. And there is no alternative to living life. It can be lived well or badly, together or apart, humanly or inhumanly. But it must be lived. It is our one mistake to assume, however, that living humanly is something that comes automatically with our existence. Human living is rather a goal to be accomplished. If human life is God's greatest work, human living is man's. It is something that has to be struggled and bargained for, captured, won, created, and protected. It comes not with birth, but with labor. It has to be won not only by each generation, but by each man. It is never wholly attained and always in great danger of being lost completely. Here is man's problem, not with the world around him or with the gods that run it, but with himself—in his struggle to become himself. His own personality and humanity is something that he must carve out for himself. If man needs God for any reason, it is to be told, not about God's worth, but about man's, not about what he is, but about what he is to become.

We have to go back to the Bible to understand how far we have wandered from the Hebrews' message about God and man. Not that the Bible is any absolute standard; it tells us that God is the only absolute. For too long we have used the Bible as a bludgeon to defeat our adversaries just as we have used the other petty absolutes of truth, dogma, and religion. The word of God is the only absolute, and that cannot be tied down to any words, formulae, or system of thought. As a result of the advance of science and knowledge, the Bible itself no longer escapes our scrutiny and suspicion. Modern theologians and historians are able to help us to understand more accurately those events in the Bible that are the basis of our faith. One thing they tell us is that the Bible is not the absolutely clear historical record it was once thought to be. The Gospels, for instance, are not eyewitness accounts of the life of Christ but rather reliable recordings of the early Christian preaching about Jesus. The opinion that the early preachers took liberties in developing their accounts of what happened in Christ's life in order to clarify the significance of that life does not weaken our historical basis of the fact of revelation.

It is to be noted that the Bible does not descend to speculation on the internal nature of God. Its presentation of God remains consistently simple and direct. It leads us to conclude that the historical man-God Jesus is all we know of God. Jesus was pleased to tell us only that God is Father. The most Christians can honestly say about God is that he is the God and Father of our Lord Jesus Christ. Any human attempts to obtain a more complete understanding of God's nature or to define that nature in human terms not only corrupts the Biblical presentation of God, but opposes what Jesus was trying to do. He came to show that God was already very much involved in the world, and that if man wants salvation he needs to get involved in the world also. We must use human words and actions to describe the nature of God's commitment to the world, but those human descriptions are always relative to the needs of the times. Our contact with the absolute comes only in terms of our own human experience or it does not come at all.

The message contained in key events of Bible history is

opposed to the use men have made of religion and other ideologies throughout history. Men use whatever is at hand to justify their positions of privilege and policies of cruelty and oppression. It is not surprising to see them enlist the services of religion for their purposes as well as the institutions of law, politics, and commerce. There is little that man can't use in his fight against man. But the one inescapable and overwhelming message the Bible offers us is that of God's full commitment to the development of our human condition. The Bible tells us that, surprisingly, God is not mad at us. He is the one person who is good, and man is the person who is bad. And the Bible uncompromisingly defines this goodness and badness in terms of man's needs and experience. The oneness and transcendence of God is presented in terms of ethics—the way men ought to get along with one another. The Bible tells men the one thing they have always suspected but never accepted: the final answer to human problems lies within them and is not to be found coming from some mysterious source outside the universe. The supernatural character of the Hebrew and Christian faith is not derived from some extraterrestrial origin but from the sudden significance given to man himself in the sacred acts of Bible history. Human happiness is no longer to be accepted as a gift from out beyond but as a human value to be created in men's dealings with one another. If God used certain historical events to attract attention to himself, it was only to direct that attention back to man himself. He stepped into our field of perception only long enough to let us know that the source of our problems rests in the way we get along with one another, not in the way he gets along with us.

The Hebrews were able to speak of their contact with God in the Exodus in terms of a covenant made by a suzerain with his vassal. Such a treaty was based upon the benevolent services performed by the suzerain in behalf of the vassal and the service of gratitude that was expected in return. One expression appearing frequently in the Old Testament describing this covenant was, "I will be your God and you will be my people." The Hebrews were impressed with the freedom and gratuity of Yahweh initiating this agreement. It was first of all a covenant of love and grace, freely given and to be freely upheld. But the agreement is conditioned by the divine requirement to obey the Law. As the great benefactor of his people, Yahweh had the right to prohibit relations with foreigners and their death-dealing gods. The first and greatest commandment is expressly: "You shall worship no other god." (EXODUS 34:14.) The second greatest commandment, similar to the first, deals with the inner health and strength of society: "You shall love your neighbor as yourself. I am the LORD." (LEVITICUS 19:18.) From his experience of the Exodus, the Hebrew was given a blinding appreciation of the benevolence of Yahweh which was to be answered by his refusal to follow other gods and to care for his brother.

It has been the tendency of religious institutions to ignore the identification of God's magnificence with the welfare of man. Too often they have set up themselves and their practices as something absolute—new false gods that have distracted from the benevolence of Yahweh. During the time of the Old Testament and ever since, organized religion has attempted to endow its positive laws with the authority of God's commands, thereby violating the whole purpose of God's commands: to free man to serve the needs of his own humanity. The Hebrews hit upon the use of codes of law as appropriate means of regulating worship and restricting the arbitrary actions of men. But their codified laws easily became ends in themselves, militating against the very freedom they were employed to support. The New Testament writers rejected the absolute and compulsive nature of Jewish law in favor of the original idea of God's covenant with his people, an order of freedom in which men feel compelled by God to serve their fellow man. For the early Christians, there was no doubt about it: rejection of the brother is the rejection of God as revealed in the resurrection of Christ. To them God had said in effect: "To worship me, serve man. Whatever does not serve man is from the worship of false gods." But it was not long before the demands of institutional religion were once more to reassert themselves in the place of God's demand. From a legitimate need to take some organized form, the church assimilated the structure of Roman law and government. Today it is still in the process of assimilating more advanced and equitable forms of law. But the message of the Bible obliges us not to worship these laws or any other laws, past or future; they are human creations and as such they can be used as obstacles or aids in the task given us by God. The strength of the church's attention to its original experience is measured by its efficiency in meeting the need of contemporary man.

It surprises people to tell them that the Bible teaches us to be good. Issues of justice and love are too simple, really, to justify the size and complexity of our religious establishment. The Bible must have some hidden and mysterious answers to be pried open with some magic tool. On the contrary, while the Bible is not always easy to understand (no mature body of literature is), its central message is quite clear and aboveboard. Man is worth man's attention. We have always been prepared to believe that we are worth God's attention, but never to accept other men as worthy of our attention. The purpose of God's revelation, the Bible, and religion is to clarify and unveil, not to mystify and obscure, man's basic need for society. The one purpose of religion is to promote the building up of the city of man according to the command of God. The one reason people reject the simplicity of the message is because it demands so much. No society in modern times has a system of law in which the interests of all people are so largely taken into account, in which the duties of rulers are so clearly expressed, and in which the crimes of the wealthy against the poor are so forcefully denounced as in the Bible. Nowhere outside the Bible is it so fundamentally stated that the welfare of society depends upon the uprightness of the citizen, not upon his status, income, affluence, or appearance. People reject the simplicity of the Bible's message for the same reason the ancients rejected the oneness of God: the Bible presents us with an ethical monotheism that brings judgment and demands a rejection of the false gods of our life. It is not that the Bible is not simple; it is too demanding. The Bible puts us into a totalitarian relationship with God that demands an unqualified obedience in the service of our neighbor.

It can safely be said today that the main concerns of the Bible are not metaphysical or theological, but ethical. The Bible makes no pretense to provide an explanation of man's nature or of God's. It goes out of its way, in fact, to point out that man's needs and God's answers are not intellectual but moral, having to do more with the direction of man's life than with the explanation of it. The drama of our salvation is being acted out on the stage of personal relationships and human happenings, not physical miracles and metaphysical changes. It has always been man's great temptation to reduce his problems to physical and metaphysical terms that are less demanding on him. Man does have physical and philosophical problems that must be faced, but these are not at the root of his specifically human problem. Christianity claims to be a historical religion, not only on the basis of its historical origin and development, but also on the basis that history itself, the total series of human events and personal interactions, is significant, revealing, and redemptive. If the Bible demands that we all take our past seriously, it is because it wants us to take our present seriously; our progress in moral interpersonal relationships demands that we know where we've been and where we should be going. Man's freedom in creating or destroying these relationships is the raw material out of which history, society, and salvation are made.

A few examples will suffice to show the predominance of ethical concerns among the basic themes of the Bible. Equity of process, the guarantee of equal protection under the law, is a basic need of society quite clearly expressed in the Bible. In spite of Yahweh's restriction on dealing with other peoples, he demanded that the foreigner living among the Hebrews be given his rights under the law:

EXODUS 12:49. "The law shall be the same for the resident alien as for the native."

EXODUS 20:10. "No work may be done then either by you, or your son or daughter, or your male or female slave, or your beast, or by the alien who lives with you."

EXODUS 22:20–22. "You shall not molest or oppress an alien, for you were once aliens yourselves in the land of Egypt. You shall not wrong any widow or orphan. If you ever wrong them and they cry out to me, I will surely hear their cry."

LEVITICUS 19:33–34. "When an alien resides with you in your land, do not molest him. You shall treat the alien who resides with you no differently than the natives born among you; have the same love for him as for yourself; for you too were once aliens in the land of Egypt. I, the LORD, am your God."

LEVITICUS 24:22. "You shall have but one rule, for alien and native alike. I, the LORD, am your God."

NUMBERS 9:14. "If an alien who lives among you wishes to keep the Lord's Passover, he too shall observe the rules and regulations for the Passover. You shall have the same law for the resident alien as for the native of the land."

NUMBERS 15:15–16. "There is but one rule for you and for the resident alien, a perpetual rule for all your descendants. Before the LORD you and the alien are alike, with the same law and the same application of it for the alien residing among you as for yourselves."

NUMBERS 15:29. "You shall have but one law for him who sins inadvertently, whether he be a native Israelite or an alien residing with you."

DEUTERONOMY 1:17. "In rendering judgment, do not consider who a person is; give ear to the lowly and to the great alike, fearing no man, for judgment is God's."

DEUTERONOMY 5:14. "No work may be done then, whether by you, or your son or daughter, or your male or female slave, or your ox or ass or any of your beasts, or the alien who lives with you. Your male and female slave should rest as you do. For remember that you too were once slaves in Egypt, and the LORD, your God, brought you from there with his strong hand and outstretched arm."

DEUTERONOMY 16:19–20. "You shall not distort justice; you must be impartial. You shall not take a bribe; for a bribe blinds the eyes even of the wise and twists the words even of the just. Justice and justice alone shall be your aim, that you may have life and may possess the land which the LORD, your God, is giving you."

JEREMIAH 7:6–7. If you no longer oppress the resident alien, the orphan, and the widow; if you no longer shed innocent blood in this place, or follow strange gods to your own harm, will I remain with you in this place, in the land which I gave your fathers long ago and forever.

JEREMIAH 22:3. Thus says the LORD: Do what is right and just. Rescue the victim from the hand of the oppressor. Do not wrong or oppress the resident alien, the orphan, or the widow, and do not shed innocent blood in this place.

MALACHI 3:5. I will draw near to you for judgment, and I will be swift to bear witness against the sorcerers, adulterers, and perjurers, those who defraud the hired man of his wages, against those who defraud widows and orphans; those who turn aside the stranger, and those who do not fear me, says the LORD of hosts.

Another example of the ethical nature of the Hebrew religion is found in the laws relating to business ethics in the Old Testament. Yahweh's concern for people was something that penetrated into their domestic and commercial life:

SIRACH 26:20; 27:1. A merchant can hardly remain upright, nor a shopkeeper free from sin; For the sake of profit many sin, and the struggle for wealth blinds the eyes.

LEVITICUS 19:13. "You shall not withhold overnight the wages of your day laborer."

DEUTERONOMY 24:14, 15. "You shall not defraud a poor and needy hired servant, whether he be one of your own countrymen or one of the aliens who live in your communities. You shall pay him each day's wages before sundown on the day itself, since he is poor and looks forward to them. Otherwise he will cry to the LORD against you, and you will be held guilty."

TOBIT 4:15. If any man hath done any work for thee, immediately pay him his hire: and let not the wages of thy hired servant stay with thee at all.

SIRACH 34:20–22. Like the man who slays a son in his father's presence is he who offers sacrifice from the possessions of the poor. The bread of charity is life itself for the needy; he who withholds it is a man of blood. He slays his neighbor who deprives him of his living; he sheds blood who denies the laborer his wages.

JEREMIAH 22:13, 17. Woe to him who builds his house on wrong, his terraces on injustice; Who works his neighbor without pay, and gives him no wages. But your eyes and heart are set on nothing except on your own gain, On shedding innocent blood, on practicing oppression and extortion.

LEVITICUS 19:35, 36. "Do not act dishonestly in using measures of length or weight or capacity. You shall have a true scale and true weights, an honest epha and an honest hin. I, the LORD, am your God, who brought you out of the land of Egypt."

DEUTERONOMY 25:13–16. "You shall not keep two differing weights in your bag, one large and the other small; nor shall you keep two different measures in your house, one large and the other small. But use a true and just weight, and a true and just measure, that you may have a long life on the land which the LORD, your God, is giving you. Everyone who is dishonest in any of these matters is an abomination to the LORD, your God."

PROVERBS 11:1. False scales are an abomination to the LORD, but a full weight is his delight.

PROVERBS 16:11. Balance and scales belong to the LORD; all the weights used with them are his concern.

PROVERBS 20:10, 23. Varying weights, varying measures, are both an abomination to the LORD. Varying weights are an abomination to the LORD, and false scales are not good.

EZEKIEL 45:9–11. Put away violence and oppression, and do what is right and just! Stop evicting my people! says the Lord GOD. You shall have honest scales, and honest epha and an honest bath. The epha and the bath shall be of the same size: the bath equal to a tenth of a homor, and the epha equal to a tenth of a homor; by the homor they shall be determined.

HOSEA 12:8–9. A merchant who holds a false balance, who loves to defraud! Though Ephraim says, "How rich I have become; I have made a fortune!" All his gain shall not suffice him for the guilt of his sin.

AMOS 8:4–6. Hear this, you who trample upon the needy and destroy the poor of the land! "When will the New Moon be over," you ask, "that we may sell our grain, and the Sabbath, that we may display the wheat? We will diminish the epha, add to the shekel, and fix our scales for cheating! We will buy the lowly man for silver, and the poor man for a pair of sandals; and even the refuse of the wheat we will sell!"

MICAH 6:10, 11. Am I to bear any longer criminal hoarding and the meager epha that is accursed? Shall I acquit criminal balances, bags of false weights?

EZEKIEL 22:12. There are those in you who take bribes to shed blood. You exact interest and usury; you despoil your neighbors violently; and me you have forgotten, says the Lord GOD.

PROVERBS 11:26. Him who monopolizes grain, the people curse—but blessings upon the head of him who distributes it!

PROVERBS 20:14. "Bad, bad!" says the buyer; but once he has gone his way, he boasts.

PROVERBS 22:16. He who oppresses the poor to enrich himself will yield up his gains to the rich as sheer loss.

SIRACH 13:21–22. Many are the supporters for a rich man when he speaks; though what he says is odious, it wins approval. When a poor man speaks they make sport of him; he speaks wisely and no attention is paid him. A rich man speaks and they say: "Who is that?" If he slips they cast him down.

SIRACH 37:7–8. Every counselor points out a way, but some counsel ways of their own; Be on the alert when one proffers advice, find out first of all what he wants. For he may be thinking of himself alone; why should the profit fall to him?

ISAIAH 10:1–2. Woe to those who enact unjust statutes and who write oppressive decrees, Depriving the needy of judgment and robbing my people's poor of their rights, Making widows their plunder, and orphans their prey!

As strong and prominent are the ethical concerns of the Old Testament, there are those even today who claim that the main concerns of religion are not ethical and that the development of the wisdom literature of the Old Testament represents a loss of appreciation for the gratuitous and historical impact of revelation. People who still regard liturgical representations of God's appearances among men as the ultimate human response to God's action are guilty of an error which was rejected by the Hebrews long before Christ. The controversy encountered by Christ was not between liturgy and ethics; there was a great body of Scripture that consistently threw its weight to the side of ethics as being the indispensable response of man to God's revelation and favor. The battle enjoined by Christ with the religious leaders and scholars of his day concerned the very nature of ethics. The Hebrews had formulated man's ethical response to God—an interpersonal, moral, and immediate response—in terms of written law. What they had accomplished was to reduce man's most human endeavor to a matter of conformity with certain legal prescriptions. Law itself became the end and norm of ethics, instead of the will of God. As much respect as Christ had for human, written law and its usefulness for the social order, he set about to topple the idol which the Hebrew leaders made of the law. Later on, St. Paul, who knew so well how close the Hebrew love for the law came to an accurate expression of man's response to revelation, condemned and equated it with sin for the very reason that it was set up in place of God, restricting a direct response to a direct offer of love.

The task of Christ was twofold: to convince people of God's goodness and to correct their response to that goodness. The world had seen great civilizations, including the Persian, Egyptian, Roman, and Jewish, built upon the paternalism of an aggrieved and demanding god. As long as men felt that they had a grievance against the gods for their woes and sufferings of life, then the leaders of the peoples could exploit the seeming inequity, assuming the paternalism of the gods they represented. The whole legal and political philosophy of the age as well as the authoritarian structure of the religions was based upon man's grand delusion concerning the hostility of the gods. If the gods were indeed just, as the more sophisticated religions taught, for some strange reason that justice never reached down to the man in the street; he experienced little of it in his life. For centuries the powers of the world existed on that assumption. There was nothing Christ could have done more to threaten and upset the political and religious balance in the world than by his simple and uncompromising insistence on the fact that God is good. He always has been, he is now, and he always will be. The resurrection appearances of Christ to his apostles and disciples left them with the compulsion to go out and tell the whole world about this good news: God loves us! And because God is love, men have the need and the capacity to love one another; it is mainly by caring for one another that they can destroy the suspicions and grievances men have against God. The revelation of God in Christ left men with the need to surrender themselves to the service of their fellow man. In their preaching they left no doubt that the life, death, and resurrection of Christ was the final revelation of God's human loving-kindness toward all men. God is not only father, he is brother. He is entirely with men, for them, within their trials, aspirations, labors, and failures. Because of this new knowledge the early Christians had of God's total commitment to man's human condition and his involvement in it, they knew they had to be with man and for man in all the situations of life.

There are three unique elements that emerge from the preaching about Christ's life: his compassionate concern for the welfare of every individual, his carefulness to attribute this same concern to his Father, and the insistence that his followers share in that concern. Commentators on the life of Christ have long extolled his capacity for entering into the problems and aspirations of those he met. He spoke directly to them, not only in terms of their understanding and experience, but in terms of their need. No need was too large or small for his consideration and response, no person too lowly or great for his encounter. Whether the official theologians needed public denouncement or the children needed the simple caress of understanding and attention, Christ was right there with an adequate and appropriate answer to the need. His great problem arose from the popular response to his matchless capacity for humanity. The great danger he faced was that the general enthusiasm his personality aroused would be directed toward himself as a man rather than toward God, leaving the people with the impression that even if God is not good, this man is. And this is exactly what happened. Instead of being reconciled to the goodness of God, the people fixed on the goodness of Christ, refusing to take the terrible leap of faith to God's own goodness. Christ's popularity aroused the suspicion and then the jealousy of the rulers, which eventually led to his death. But what threatened the leaders most of all was his disregard for the law. This was their vested interest, their hold on the people, their means of security and prestige. Once the law was dethroned as the be-all of religion, their status within the community would be destroyed; this they understood well. Once people were brought into contact with an ethical god and once the demands of ethics preceded the demands of the law, then a religion based on law would come crumbling down. The doctrine that God is really man's brother and friend must be squelched; any human being who claims to be God's son is really above the law and must be cut down. Christ came to claim that not only is he God's son, but all men are. Those who believe this have been cut down ever since. But it was only with the resurrection appearances of Christ that the apostles and their followers were able to accept the truth that what Christ stood for, God stands for: God was in Christ reconciling the whole world to himself. The dynamic thrust of the Christian movement ever since and the bursts of renewal that bring it back to life are all derived from the intimacy of man's fellowship with God which defies and puts down all the authorities of the world. Reconciliation with God's goodness means battle with all the petty tyrants of the world warring against man's welfare.

The New Testament teaches us that the experience of God's immediate goodness in Christ must be translated into immediate and concrete concern for the good of the brother. This is not just the best response, it is the only one. Paul tells us that Christianity is not made up of doctrine or system, a superior tradition of theology or mystical rites, great acts of heroism or self-immolation, but rather the simple act of sharing the life and concerns of the brother:

> Charity is patient, is kind; charity does not envy, is not pretentious, is not puffed up, is not ambitious, is not self-seeking, is not provoked; thinks no evil, does not rejoice over wickedness, but rejoices with the truth; bears all things, believes all things, hopes all things, endures all things. I CORINTHIANS 13:4–7.

The fraternal love of Christ for every person who came to his attention, in his teaching, his acts of encouragement and support, his miracles and healings, and his death-for-us, was at one and the same time a manifestation of God's love and a pattern for our own. The ability to take up the burdens and joys of others is not only man's most divine prerogative, it is God's.

The records of the apostles' teachings leave no doubt about it: our faith in God's goodness is measured by the immediacy and practicality of our concern for others. The particularism and pervasive relevance of Hebrew law was to be replaced by the still more demanding variation and contingency of human need: "For I say to you that unless your justice exceeds that of the Scribes and Pharisees, you shall not enter the kingdom of heaven." (MATTHEW 5:20.) So particular are the demands of God in each situation in which we find others, that Christ was reluctant to teach by just giving principles, but preferred giving object lessons from which his listeners could draw insights to match their own situations. This method of teaching ethics by story is in fact the most effective way of bringing the goodness of God to bear on the countless and unpredictable situations of life. Instead of merely giving an exhortation on purity of motive, thereby making it an end in itself, Christ said all that needed to be said in this description:

> "Therefore when thou givest alms, do not sound a trumpet before thee, as the hypocrites do in the synagogues and streets, in order that they may be honored by men. Amen I say to you, they have received their reward. But when thou givest alms, do not let thy left hand know what thy right hand is doing, so that thy alms may be given in secret; and thy Father, who sees in secret, will reward thee." MATTHEW 6:2–4.

The primacy of ethics over the concerns of law and liturgy were taught in the following graphic pronouncements:

"Therefore, if thou art offering thy gift at the altar, and there rememberest that thy brother has anything against thee, leave thy gift before the altar and go first to be reconciled to thy brother, and then come and offer thy gift." MATTHEW 5:23–24.

"What man is there among you who, if he has a single sheep and it falls into a pit on the Sabbath, will not take hold of it and lift it out? How much better is a man than a sheep! Therefore, it is lawful to do good on the Sabbath." MATTHEW 12:11–12.

The arrival of God's kingdom on earth was announced first in the good works of Christ, secondly in the good works of his apostles:

And Jesus was going about all the towns and villages, teaching in their synagogues, and preaching the gospel of the kingdom, and curing every kind of disease and infirmity. But seeing the crowds, he was moved with compassion for them, because they were sheep without a shepherd. Then he said to his disciples, "The harvest indeed is great, but the laborers are few. Pray therefore the Lord of the harvest to send forth laborers into his harvest." MATTHEW 9:35–38.

But when John had heard in prison of the works of Christ, he sent two of his disciples to say to him, "Art thou he who is to come, or shall we look for another?" And Jesus answering said to them, "Go and report to John what you have heard and seen: the blind see, the lame walk, the lepers are cleansed, the dead rise, the poor have the gospel preached to them. And blessed is he who is not scandalized in me." MATTHEW 11:2–6.

"Come to me, all you who labor and are burdened, and I will give you rest. Take my yoke upon you, and learn from me, for I am meek and humble of heart; and you will find rest for your souls. For my yoke is easy and my burden light." MATTHEW 11:28–30.

"But I say to you who are listening: Love your enemies, do good to those who hate you. Bless those who curse you, pray for those who calumniate you. And to him who strikes thee on the one cheek, offer the other also; and from him who takes away thy cloak, do not withhold thy tunic either. Give to everyone who asks of thee, and from him who takes away thy goods, ask no return. And even as you wish men to do to you, so also do you to them. And if you love those who love you, what merit have you? For even sinners love those who love them. But love your enemies and do good, and lend, not hoping for any return, and your reward shall be great, and you shall be children of the Most High, for he is kind towards the ungrateful and evil. Be merciful, therefore, even as your Father is merciful." LUKE 6:27–32, 35–36.

"But why do you call me, 'Lord, Lord,' and not practice the things I say? Everyone who comes to me and hears my words and acts upon them, I will show you what he is like." LUKE 6:46–47.

"But when thou givest a feast, invite the poor, the crippled, the lame, the blind; and blessed shalt thou be, because they have nothing to repay thee with; for thou shalt be repaid at the resurrection of the just." LUKE 14:13–14.

"I am the good shepherd, and I know mine and mine know me, even as the Father knows me and I know the Father; and I lay down my life for my sheep. And other sheep I have that are not of this fold. Them also I must bring, and they shall hear my voice, and there shall be one fold and one shepherd." JOHN 10:14–16.

"Do you know what I have done to you? You call me Master and Lord, and you say well, for so I am. If, therefore, I the Lord and Master have washed your feet, you also ought to wash the feet of one another. For I have given you an example, that as I have done to you, so you also should do." JOHN 13:13–15.

"A new commandment I give you, that you love one another: that as I have loved you, you also love one another. By this will all men know that you are my disciples, if you have love for one another." JOHN 13:34–35.

In this we have come to know his love, that he laid down his life for us; and we likewise ought to lay down our life for the brethren. He who has the goods of this world and sees his brother in need and closes his heart to him, how does the love of God abide in him? My dear children, let us not love in word, neither with the tongue, but in deed and in truth. I JOHN 3:16–18.

But Jesus had to die. No system of his time could tolerate the idea of a benevolent and ethical god. It would put too much strain on the paternal and totalitarian structures. These demanded a faith which the people were not able to have in themselves; the reason they could not have this faith in themselves was that they had no faith in the goodness of God. And when God is against a person, the only thing left to do is submit to the blandishments of whatever other god comes along. But put Christ to death they did, and strangely enough they put to death along with him God and all he stood for until then. With Christ was put to death all the divinities of the world who still attempt to tyrannize over men, and all those who pretend to divinity in order to exploit their fellow men. With Christ died all the fears, guilt, anxiety, and grievance against God with which men had attempted to worship God until his time. With him died also the pretensions of philosophy, law, politics, art, and science to provide the final word on questions of man's destiny and happiness. With Christ died all of man's idols.

And with Christ there arose a new image of God, a God-brother, God with us and for us. Christ would be with us no longer in his flesh in order to emphasize that God is with us always in our own flesh. There will be no more danger of attributing to Christ, or any other person or system or idea, the compassion and initial approachability that belong to God. We no longer gather around Christ; we live in his spirit. If we want to touch and feel God, to serve him, we have only to approach our neighbor. The only thing necessary, now that God has shown us his love in the life, death, and resurrection of Christ, is that we love one another.

CHAPTER TWO

A Church for People

Christ did away with religion by showing us that God is at man's side, not over his head. The world we live in is not a vertical, up-and-down world with God at the top and a niche for each of us somewhere below on the scale. It is strictly a horizontal world with everything built for man's wide-angle vision. Man only gets stiff-necked trying to look up all the time. If he is going to meet his creator at all, it has to be in the across-the-room relationship he has with his neighbor and the rest of the world. Christ's God is totally ethical, that is, to be met and known only in this horizontal world of human interpersonal relationships. Whatever demands there are in religion apart from the demands of human needs do not come from God but from some pretender. Because God has so completely identified himself with man's need, religion is ethics. God serves man; so must man.

Even though Christ did away with religion, he needed a church, an antireligious church, if you will. We really don't live in a vertical and authoritarian world, although people once thought that we do. Because of the fact that the sun seems to be up and parents seem to be smarter than their children, people have nearly always considered the universe to be structured on the same pattern, with better things up, worse things down, older people smarter, and newer people dumb. So ingrained is this view of things, and so pervasive is man's grievance against what he thinks is an unfriendly god, that Christ couldn't just tell us that the opposite was true and let it go at that. He had to show us that the demands of ethics and God's commitment to them go so far as laying down one's life for the brethren. And he needed a group of people to keep his dying alive, to show all people everywhere that God's glory consists in sharing man's inadequacy. Christ wants all men to know that they are God's people, his church, his friends, and companions-on-the-way. He walks with them, not on top of them. What Christ was after, really, was a group of people that would be an antichurch that could war on the false idols and the death-dealing ideologies and religions that would distract from the service of God's brothers. He needed some people to go out and tell the world the good news that nothing is worthy of man's worship except God, and he has deferred to man. Christ needed some practical and sensible people who knew what life and work were all about, men who were too sensible ever to have any pretensions to power or privilege. He found what he needed in some Palestinian fishermen.

So down-to-earth were these men that they were hard to take away from their work; they all seemed to be in a good business, they knew it well, and they enjoyed it. Their unclerical attitudes toward everything were just what Christ wanted. The last thing that he wanted to do was to make clerics and religious persons out of them. He founded the first "unseminary"; he took his company around the country pointing out the many different needs other people had and showed them how to meet those needs. Tampering with nothing in their capacity for humanity and individuality, he developed it and opened it to greater enrichment. Whenever they thought they could start pontificating, he slapped down that ambition with dispatch:

"The Scribes and the Pharisees have sat on the chair of Moses. All things, therefore, that they command you, observe and do. But do not act according to their works; for they talk but do nothing. And they bind together heavy and oppressive burdens, and lay them on men's shoulders; but not with one finger of their own do they choose to move them." MATTHEW 23:2–4.

And they said, "Grant to us that we may sit, one at thy right hand and the other at thy left hand, in thy glory." But Jesus said to them, "You do not know what you are asking for. Can you drink of the cup of which I drink, or be baptized with the baptism with which I am to be baptized?" MARK 10:37–38.

Now a discussion arose among them, which of them was the greatest. But Jesus, knowing the reasoning of their heart, took a little child and set him at his side, and said to them, "Whoever receives this little child for my sake, receives me; and whoever receives me, receives him who sent me. For he who is the least among you, he is the greatest." But John answered and said, "Master, we saw a man casting out devils in thy name, and we forbade him, because he does not follow with us." And Jesus said to him, "Do not forbid him; for he who is not against you is for you." And they went and entered a Samaritan town to make ready for him; and they did not receive him, because his face was set for Jerusalem. But when his disciples James and John saw this, they said, "Lord, wilt thou that we bid fire come down from heaven and consume them?"

But he turned and rebuked them, saying, "You do not know of what manner of spirit you are; for the Son of Man did not come to destroy men's lives, but to save them." LUKE 9:46–50, 52–56.

In the resurrection and the reception of the Holy Spirit, the apostles finally got the message: Christ was the revelation of God's being with and for man. Domination was out, service in. The first Christians were so taken up by this that they were not able to contain themselves. The apostles expressed it in their mission of preaching, the more erudite in their ministry of teaching, the unlearned in the joyous blabbering of the gift of tongues, the heroic in the witness of martyrdom, and all Christians in solicitude for the needy. Christ had freed man for his human tasks; the concerns of real people had been validated as the final concerns of God. Man was now the topic of religion. The early church set out to embrace man in his need according to the image of God in Christ. The Christian church was, in its love feasts, its fraternal concern for all, and in its sufferings, the picture of what all mankind would someday be. The early Christian knew that the care and reverence he received from others in the church would some day be experienced by all men; he was in the place where all people would be on the last day. In those early years of great suffering and fresh excitement, Christ's unchurchly church was the sign of what the world would become, the workshop of man's greatest creation: his own humanity.

I say the church *was*. No longer does it serve the flesh loved and cherished by God as his own. For a long time it has disdained the aspirations and strivings of men. For centuries the greatest obstacle to human progress has been the church itself. In its tremendous organizational potential and investment, the church today remains immobile and resistant to the movement of man. Any gesture it makes simulating an awakening from the centuries-long coma it has suffered creates a storm of interest among men. Any movement in its giant but sclerotic limbs evokes accolades of applause and recognition. Most people choose to ignore its comatose condition; but it wears down on them, nevertheless, an enormous parasite draining their energy and tolerance. The reformers and physicians have tried several times to wake it up, and the present efforts also seemed doomed to failure for the same reasons as earlier ones. It is not only the world's humanity the church fails to take seriously, but its own humanity. The disease consists not in being too human, but not human enough.

Most Catholics are embarrassed by the humanity of the church. Too bad, they say, God had to use us to do his work. People are that part of the church we just have to put up with. The human element in the church is responsible for everything wrong in the church, in contrast to the divine element, which is incorruptible, victorious, triumphant. To the human element we ascribe all the failures of the church: bad popes, drunken pastors, resistance to human progress, delay in reform. Don't blame the church, because it is only human. Yet don't change the church, because it is divine. The human element is the church's enormous and messy back yard. Don't talk about it; other people have messy back yards too. No need in even trying to clean it up. The task would be too vast and ponderous. Instead, we will keep the front up nice. Not that the supernatural destroys the natural in us, it just sits on it a little. The church really doesn't need any reform (that implies that something is wrong with it!). What it needs is only more of the same spiritual remedies that we have neglected to use in recent years: missions, retreats, self-denial, and resignation to pain and hardship. These made men out of our forebears and will do the same for us.

The need for human satisfaction is not really very important—in the church, certainly. What if we never get anything out of worship? We are not supposed to! It's what we give that counts. What if we wear ourselves out in parish activities that never seem to change anything but only keep it all the same? We are serving the Lord, and that's all that matters. What if the church has no answers to the problems of marriage and sex today? The suffering and anxiety caused by this indifference are good for us, shortening our time in purgatory. What if our parish is not very involved in the problems of the community at large? The aims of the church are primarily spiritual and not social. What if our clergy build fancy rectories and communication systems that only aid them in not communicating with those they were ordained to serve? You don't expect our secular priests to get involved in the secular? Their mission is a universal one and cannot descend into the particularities of the temporal sphere. We don't want our priests getting mixed up in any causes. If they are interested in them, they can serve them best by not being directly involved and thereby losing their acceptability. The priest has to be a mystical sign to the world of Christ's Second Coming, whatever that is. If our priests are remote from the tragedy of human life, well, so is God. Religion is for God, and he is separate. If our nuns and priests and holy people isolate themselves from the rest of men, it is only because they want to be closer to God. Separation is the only way we can preserve our religion pure and undefiled, as the Jews did. To be separate and different is to be Catholic. Catholic schools, Catholic bowling teams, Catholic artists, Catholic sales—that's our way. To be separated from our bodies is the final release we are all getting ready for, and others could do no better than get ready for it too. Human needs? They are not important, except as a means of attracting attention to religion. Human satisfaction? Bad, as an end in itself. Death? It's the beginning of our real life, in which we will no longer be bothered with the contingencies and variations of our humanity.

The foregoing expression of cynicism is a product of the ingrown concerns of the church. At one time the church was the gadfly of secular society, urging it on to fully realize its potential. At one time the church carried on the work of Christ as the ethical leader and prophet of the world. At one time the church was fully with the world as it felt God was. But no longer. What concerns the church now is not the advance of mankind, but merely the perpetuation of its own institutions. The church has set itself up as a new god, a new end-in-itself, with all the appurtenances and privileges of a past age, to be worshiped and served by all men. To serve the church, to observe its protocol, to subscribe to its discipline, to perform its ceremonies, to support its pastors, to obey its precepts, and to pray its prayers is salvation. No matter how little one gets out of it (and it is true that many clerics and bishops get as little out of it as anybody else), he still has the satisfaction of serving the church, and the church is God's even if he isn't. The suspension of one's own need for satisfaction in favor of the demands of the church is a good and heroic thing. At one time God stood with all men, individually and collectively; now he stands only with the institution called the church. Man is no longer obliged to die for his fellow man but for the church. One's fellow man isn't worth it any more.

Perhaps the self-consciousness suffered by the church today is a result of its identification with a certain political philosophy. For nearly three centuries the church was apolitical. Christ had refused to align himself with any political party or social theory; for him man's need was the only absolute by which political systems and theories should be judged. He said love your neighbor; whatever kind of action your neighbor's need demands, give it to him. If it can be met by one alone, fine. But if his needs are so complex that they demand the action of several people together or of a whole state, then it must be done. Conversely, whatever man as a group needs, that service the individual must render. God stands with man as an individual, group, a class. Love your neighbor, Jesus said, and and do what is appropriate.

The political attitude of the early church was one of fierce independence. People began to take care of one another in defiance of the regulations of the god-almighty state. The hostility of the early Christians to their governments is well known. Because they refused to bow down and worship any human authority, institution, or political system, they were branded as atheists, as indeed they were. Because they refused to be herded into the recognized places of worship and preferred instead to gather in their homes for their simple meals of fellowship, they were dragged before the courts and condemned as agitators and nonconformists. Because of their complete indifference to the demands and threats of the state and their recourse to a higher law than the Roman one, they were beaten and thrown to the lions. As Christ before them, they died for claiming to be, and acting like, the children of God. These were the explosively nonviolent and passively resistant days of the church; uncommitted to anything except human need and suffering, they portrayed the humanity of God in a demonstration that has never been equaled since.

The Empire finally capitulated to Christian persistence. No need fighting an enemy like that, thought Constantine; and so he made Christianity the official religion of the Empire. A remarkable transfer took place in the church. The dignity and independence that once belonged to the individual by his faith in God now were attributed to the church as a privileged institution. In a closed society, the only possible avenue of institutional existence is state recognition and patronage. The bishops of the church thought that they had worked out a good deal, even though it was the emperor who had called the terms. It was the emperor who called the councils and dismissed the bishops and settled the disputes. But the new subservience of the church was going to pay off. In the West it had gained some institutional autonomy; it was in a position to rise from the status of the mistress of secular society to that of master. As the barbarian hordes came bulldozing down from the north and leveling the monuments of antiquity, the church was there to welcome them. Agile and suitably equipped with the tools of Roman law and philosophy, the church began its conquest of these newly arrived children. Having survived the destruction of the old civilization, it became the supervisor in charge of building the new. As this metamorphosis of secular society took place, the church grew and finally emerged as something entirely new: a completely separate society. Now there were two societies, civil and ecclesiastical. Each had its own law and court system, each had its own source of revenue and own membership. Persons belonged either to one society or the other. If one belonged to the church, he was either a cleric or a religious brother or nun. Members of civil society were laymen. Originally the church was in the world and with it. Then it gradually became the church and the world. Finally it was the church apart from the world, opposed to it.

Along with the structural changes of the church occasioned by the demands of history, corresponding theological changes naturally took place. The authoritarian and paternalistic images once rejected by the church were now adopted by it. Faced with the illiteracy and symbolic consciousness of the barbarians, the vertical image of reality suddenly became meaningful to the church. Primitive Old Testament concepts of God were applied to Christ, the invincible conqueror of nations. To be saved meant to give one's allegiance to Christ and support his vicars-on-earth. The loss of Christ's humanity—a process begun with the absorption of Greek philosophy—was tempered by the introduction of the new mediators: Mary and the saints. A front-office religion was set up that outlawed access to the Almighty. One must always approach God through the right combination of intercessors: the church, the clergy, the sacraments, the saints, and their images and relics. Jesus had come to tell man he has no need for a mediating religion: "In that day you shall ask in my name; and I do not say to you that I will ask the Father for you, for the Father himself loves you because you have loved me, and have believed that I came forth from God." (JOHN 16:26–27.) Now the church had constructed a whole pantheon of mediators and intercessors.

Slowly the church would come back to an appreciation of the humanity of Christ. The Franciscan school of theology, the modern school of piety, the exercises of Ignatius of Loyola, and the many devotions to the suffering Christ were gropings for a more humanitarian religion. But it was the task of Martin Luther and the early reformers to firmly re-establish the humanity of Christ and his union with mankind. But while the Protestants applied New Testament concepts of God to Christ, the political situation did not warrant the application of those concepts to God. That is a task left up to our day. Although the church has made great strides in the last few years in taking seriously the concerns of man, it has not yet attained the intensity of concern that belonged to the early church. It cannot accept the brotherhood of man without a strong belief in the brotherhood of God.

The opposition of church and state theoretically came to an end with the American Revolution. This was by no means a religious war or an essentially anticlerical one. But the political situation that arose out of it was a unique one for the church, one it has not yet accepted. The new situation of the church grew out of the demands of nationalism, the need for unity among peoples of different religions, and the doctrinaire humanism of the times. With the Declaration of Independence and Bill of Rights, the privilege and independence that had belonged to the church since the time of Constantine were transferred back to the individual. This time it is not faith, but legal guarantees of personal freedom that set the individual over and against the society in which he lives and the forces with which he must contend. The church now finds itself in the situation in which its freedom no longer depends upon its privileges as an institution before the state, but upon the freedoms guaranteed by the state to the individual in a free society. The independence of the church now results from the freedom of the citizen to assemble, think, speak, and do as he well pleases. The church, as a result, finds itself in competition with the thousand other organizations that arise from man's freedom to take care of his own needs. The church is one voice among many offering something to the citizens of secular society; it may no longer conduct itself as if it were a perfect society, self-sufficient and self-regulatory. It is now just one voluntary society among many other voluntary societies. People are free to join and leave the church as their conscience dictates. The whole problem of church and state is a false problem, no more a problem than Elks and state or the Community Chest and state. The only problem faced by the church in a free society is whether it has the courage to divest itself completely of the privileges of an age long gone in order to utilize the new freedom at its disposal. Extolling the glory and status of the past, it is wasting the opportunities of the present. The effectiveness of the church today depends on its ability to forego its medieval fixation on privilege and join the rest of the human race. If it does, it has the chance of becoming Christian once more and revealing the God of Christ to men.

The freedoms of our American society have never been fully realized or secured; they are always in danger of slipping out of our hands. The gods of tyranny and oppression still have great power. In our own country they have taken the form of the military-industrial complex which appears to dominate more and more of our life. Church and state are among the many institutional vassals giving obeisance to the god of business. The schools of our country have rapidly become business establishments serving the needs of commerce and industry. The church has not only aligned itself with the interests of business, but it has subscribed to the ethics of business, employing more and more the techniques and values of successful corporations. In exchange for its servitude and complaisance, it has been granted the privilege of building tax-exempt churches and running its own educational system. In its anxiety to retain its prestige and defend its patriotism, it has exchanged its heritage of prophetical freedom for a mess of bricks and mortar. In spite of its gothic structure and Roman liturgy, the church comes up looking and sounding like an American business, the creature of our industrial feudalism.

The ecclesiastical doctors and reformers probing the comatose body of the church have not yet come up with an accurate diagnosis. From the pens of theologians and

Council Fathers come more words about asserting the divinity of the church, modifying its forms to reveal more clearly its divine constitution, emphasizing the need for interior renewal instead of external changes, and presenting the church as the mystery of Christ in the world. But the problem with the church is not that it is not sufficiently divine. It is not sufficiently human. The problem of the church is not that it is not relevant to the world; it is too relevant to the interests of some and not at all to the interests of others. The problem is that the church is not relevant to the God of the New Testament who is with the needs and concerns of all in our society. The problem is not so much that the church has taken the form of a business corporation, but that it has not also taken many other familiar forms as well. The problem is, finally, not so much what the structures of the church are in the modern world, but what is the church's task in it. If the church were to have a clear set of concerns, then it would have some guidelines for setting up new structures. But as long as the concern of our theologians, liturgists, and reformers consists merely in articulating their concept of the divinity of the church, they miss out on the humanity of God.

The task of Christians, individually and collectively, is to bear witness to God's love for man by means of their own practical love for man. This comes not only by preaching, but especially in the doing. The task of the church, then, is to promote the building of the city of man according to its belief in the brotherhood of God. The essential task of the church is one and multiple at the same time; it is as simple and complex as human need. The activities and roles of the church must change with the contingencies of human need. While the church does need concrete forms of political organization, those forms cannot be tied down to any set or lasting pattern; they depend on the type of action that is called forth by the demands of human need. Whatever solutions are available to human problems, those the church must be ready to support. The concrete needs of man are the mediators of God's will to the church.

What the church becomes depends upon its activities. Its activities depend on its ultimate concerns. And its concerns depend ultimately on its idea of God. The reform of the church depends on how Christian it allows its God to be.

The church is not 100 per cent human. But it should be. Whatever is in it that is not human is not of God. The church was founded to be a model of humanity to man. People should be able to see in the church what their own lives are to become. The modern false prophets who speak of the tension that should exist between the world and the church have missed the point. The church is here to support and promote what is most human in men, to aid and encourage what is most promising in society, to applaud freedom and whatever furthers it, and to bring out the best in the world. Certainly there will be tension between a Christian church and the culture in which it lives, not between the church and what is human in that culture, but what is inhuman and less than human. The Christian is to wage war on whatever militates against the human in himself, the church, and secular society. The good news is not one of judgment, least of all on the church, but one of supreme and undeniable validation of what we are and what we want to be. The church's own humanity is not its cross but its greatest and only asset. Only by portraying, in its teaching, customs, worship, and secular concerns, what each culture can and must be—in terms each culture can understand and absorb—will the church present the God of Christ to men. But if the church remains aloof to any human value or need, it bears witness to the aloofness and indifference of God. But if it can take them to heart and act upon them, becoming all things to all men, then it will grow in its own humanity, and God will become real for the world.

The task of Christians is not to bring God to the world—

as if God were not already there, or waiting for our concern before he became involved! God is mightily at work performing his wonders in the world, sharing man's great exploits in science, government, education, and communications. We are living in an age of great revolution, and God is in the midst of the fray leading his hosts, as always, against the demons of inequity, ignorance, hunger, poverty, and pain. God is right there in the councils of government, the bargaining sessions of labor and management, the laboratories of technology, the operating room, the offices of business, and the family parlors. His great delight is to share in the pertinent decisions and insights that build up the family of man. Whatever opens up the channels of thought and communication, whatever makes people one with themselves and one another, and whatever heals man's deformities and reconciles him to his neighbor is the work of God in the world. The most unsuspecting and unreligious instruments are used by God to work his greatest miracles today, miracles that outclass anything we read of in the Bible. The accomplishments of the industrial and economic revolutions were outdone by the revolutions of chemistry, electronics, and communication. The newest and most important revolution of all has just begun, the human revolution, in which man himself has come under the open gaze of science. Will the church continue to stand back as a guardian of its past while the struggle for a human world pushes on? Or will it be able to come to its senses, gather its strength, mobilize its forces, seek out the enemies, and throw itself into the world where God is? Unless the church finds God in the world, it won't find him at all. And unless the church finds him, nobody else will. God is out there in the world. For the church, it's in to be out.

CHAPTER THREE

Building the Kingdom

An articulate friend of mine recently presented his church with a two-point program for parish renewal:

1) Abolish churchgoing.
2) Burn down the parish church.

Until we can bring ourselves to think in terms such as these, we are merely playing the devil's game. All of our efforts of reform and reunion are futile unless we have grasped the simple fact that the church is people and therefore something *to be* rather than *to go to*. I personally had often thought of giving church buildings back to the community in compensation for not paying taxes on church property. But the ceremony of burning down the parish church and school would be a much more Christian oblation. It would dramatically represent a real conversion to serve the living God and a rejection of the worship of the brick-and-mortar monuments we have erected in every corner of the land. Our addiction to the construction narcotic surpasses all other ecclesiastical aberrations. A spot check at the local chancery office will indicate that eight out of ten visitors are there to arrange for the purchase or sale of something. There is a veritable parade of salesmen, architects, contractors, and pastors beleaguered by the conspiracy. The church in America has sold its birthright of freedom for a mess of pottage—the ability to raise funds, lay concrete, bless walls, and spread floor wax. Where can we find a cure for this hod-carrying syndrome?

A good place to look is the Bible. The New Testament tells us that salvation is not found in the building of temples or in religious rites:

Do not be led away by various and strange doctrines. For it is good to make steadfast the heart by grace, not by foods, in which those who walked found no profit. We have an altar, from which they have no right to eat who serve the tabernacle. For the bodies of those animals whose blood is brought into the Holies by the high priest for sin, are burned outside the camp; and so Jesus also, that he might sanctify the people by his blood, suffered outside the gate. Let us therefore go to him outside the camp, bearing his reproach; for here we have no permanent city, but we seek for the city that is to come. Through him, therefore, let us offer up a sacrifice of praise always to God, that is, fruit of lips praising his name. And do not forget kindness and charity, for by such sacrifices God's favor is obtained. HEBREWS 13:10–16.

There are plenty of halls and school buildings available for Christians to meet in—at considerably less cost than now spent to operate their own buildings. Being without property would be an exciting expression of our eschatology, looking forward to, and working for, the more perfect city that is to come. If the church is to do its job, it has to start camping out in the world where Christ is.

But not having churches to build and schools to run, what is the church going to do? The answer is simply that we will have to find out. The activities of the church depend on what its concerns are. Once the church has identified with the needs of men and has dedicated itself to the building of the city of man according to the command of Christ, it is likely that its activities will become as rich and varied as human experience itself. The forms, programs, and structures of the church will take the shape of the church's new concerns.

The one commodity the church has to offer the world is ethics. In ethics man contacts the God revealed in Christ. The labor of the church should be directed toward the promotion of justice—justice in government, management, and labor, justice in distribution of property and the means of production, justice in business, law enforcement, community life, and group relations, justice in technology, science, medicine, and communications, justice in the family and personal relations, and finally justice within man himself. Secular society looks to the church for ethical guidance. The church should be the one organization identified with man in his most human need: self-determination. This priority gives the church the authority and responsibility to aid men in what ought to be done. The other organizations of the world all serve lesser needs. It is up to the church to point out and promote the changing ethical needs of men. The church alone can bring the law of Christ into contact with the activities of men.

There are still some in the church today who reject the church's involvement in the secular. They speak of the new imperialism of the church; they view with great suspicion the presence of pastors on community welfare councils, priests in politics, and nuns in picket lines. The clergy, they say, should allow the lay people to directly involve themselves in the secular. Priests should dispense the sacraments and the word of God and wait until the lay people have sufficiently prepared the ground before they venture into the secular fray. The claim is made that priests are not competently enough trained in sociology, psychology, and community planning to involve themselves in matters that should be left up to experts. The secular is the arena for lay action, not for clerical intrusion.

This thinking represents several theological errors. The first denies the authority of priests and prelates to lead the Christian people. You don't lead people by pushing them on ahead of you. A leader needs a certain amount of perspective, but this comes mainly by involvement, not by isolation resulting from a desire for objectivity. In matters of human relationships, there is no such thing as objectivity or neutrality; one is either on one side or the other. To refuse to be involved puts one on one side or the other. Silence and indifference are the most effective kinds of involvement, often the most destructive. Refusal by the clergy to do anything about a situation is *already* to have done something about it.

The clergy enter the secular field as amateurs in many matters for which they should seek out expert guidance. They must not allow their competence in theological matters or their prestige within the group or community to be taken for competence in nonreligious fields. But they are competent in the matters of justice and ethics. But their competence in a particular case demands that they be within the situation and not pontificate their decisions from outside. They must become involved in the situation if they are to identify with the needs of people and bring effective ethical leadership to bear upon them. The only objectivity allowable in human problems is the subjective experience of the situation itself. If the clergy are prohibited that experience, they will continue to dictate on matters with which they are not familiar.

The keep-the-clergy-out thinking denies the secular orientation of the church. If the clergy are not allowed to give real leadership in ethical concerns, then those ethical concerns will not be considered primary concerns of the church. Unless the priests give effective leadership in love, there will be no action in love by the church membership. There are not two churches or two love-ethics, one for the clergy and one for the lay people. The most effective way to keep the church from fulfilling its task of promoting the kingdom of God is to confine priests to the sanctuary and rectory. The one thing that must not be done to leadership is to sit on it. To deny that leadership access to the secular denies the commitment of the church to the world. To do that denies the commitment of God to the world. The first thing that must be done to equip the church for its task is to desacralize the priesthood so that it may shoulder its burden of Christian leadership.

But the task of the church goes much further than freeing the clergy for their task. It must educate the whole Christian people for involvement. This means a lot more than not getting excited when Father is seen on the platform or in the picket line. It means turning people's hearts to the needs of others, a lifelong process. Whatever can be used to develop qualities of courage, compassion, kindness, and dedication is valuable to Christian education. Whatever makes people fighting mad about an injustice and leads them to do something about it is Christian leadership.

The greatest contribution of the church to the world's ethical progress will be made by individual Christians in their own jobs and spheres of influence. The biggest impact will be made by competent men doing their job well, not by formally organized church programs. The example of President Kennedy can be cited as a truly Christian act of witness. He gave more ethical leadership to this country than twenty years of bishops' statements and priests' sermons. He was an effective politician first of all. He had great qualities of heart and soul secondly. He was the product of a thoroughly American and Christian tradition; he could speak directly to the felt needs of his time. He gave great relevance and meaning to the term "Catholic layman"; he remains a great model for all men to follow. He provided the church with a great cue to its task of religious formation.

The kingdom of God is human society. The foundation of this kingdom is the human person. He is the one with whom God stands, not with any ideology, institution, or organization. God serves his needs and puts himself at his disposal. All other human creations—dogmas, philosophies, cultures, and governments—are relative in value to the needs of the individual person. Since man is a secular creature, his needs are all secular. For this reason the Christian love-ethic is a secular ethic. Man does not have the option of renouncing his earthly nature and secular needs. Even his most spiritual and noble needs arise from his concrete and existential situation; he may renounce some needs in favor of others, but they are all earthy, defined by his relationship to the real. Even man's religious needs are secular, coming from his creatureliness. His approach to God can only be in terms of this creatureliness. God's approach to man can only be in terms of that same creatureliness. Unless God is supremely good in relation to man's secular needs, man has no reason for loving him. Revelation is considered supernatural, not because it is unsecular, but because without God's gratuitous intervention in the affairs of men they would never know of his inscrutable goodness-for-man. Christ came to tell us that God takes us seriously, as we are in our human condition. He validated the earthiness of that condition and told us we have to take it seriously too. God loves the world. Matter matters.

The surprising thing about God's kingdom is not that it is entirely of God's own making. People never doubted that God rules over his own dominions. But what was surprising was the revelation that the kingdom was to be of man's own making as well, that man's city is God's enterprise. The earth is God's dominion. God came into the world not to relieve man of his earthly condition, but to direct him to it, not to make man God, but to make man *man*, to develop his humanity.

As the secular needs of the individual are the object of God's concern, so they should be of the church's concern. In turn, it is the church's task to make man's secular needs the concern of secular society. Society becomes God's kingdom to the extent that it becomes a community of *persons*, where the worth of the individual is regarded as a primary value and his needs as ultimate concerns. Men are coming to reject the common good as being some kind of ideal organizational pattern to which all the citizens must conform. Too often, what is passed off as this ideal is merely the combination of the interests of a certain group of people, a philosophical pretext used by one group to exploit another. The common good is rather the greatest possible good for the greatest number of individuals. The good of society is identified with the good of the individual person. It is the task of others in society to aid the individual in the appreciation and realization of his own needs. The fact that each individual is a son of God, his own king, his own pope, and his own teacher is the basic doctrine that the Bible offers the development of society.

The first job of the church is to make men out of people. It must teach them to take themselves seriously. But to do this, they must take society seriously. They can only become what their condition and environment allow them to become. Man's ability to perfect himself is limited greatly by the economic, social, and political situation in which he lives. If he is to obtain what he needs, he must often organize, associate with others who have the same ideas and needs, and use corporate strength and pressure to meet those needs.

This is why the church should be doctrinally committed to social action. Individual dignity is meaningless without the right and ability to utilize common interests to promote that dignity. There is no individual need, even the unique and most personal, that cannot be better served through group action. The proliferation and freedom of groups—clubs, organizations, corporations, trade and industrial unions, and political parties—are a sign of a strong acceptance of individual dignity and the variety of forms it must take. Those most interested in themselves are those most involved in group work of some kind. Perhaps the most characteristic expression of the Christian doctrine of salvation has been the need for free assembly. The persistence of Christians throughout the centuries in their practice of gathering for worship in spite of persecution has been a great force in the development of a free society. The faith that sees every man as God's brother demands that minority groups be allowed to grow and propagate, that minority opinions be given the opportunity of becoming majority opinions, and that people be allowed to assemble to satisfy their own needs.

One important precedent justifying the church's promotion of social action was its support of unionism. It is to the great credit of the church that it played a vital role in the development of collective bargaining in this country, certainly one of the major social developments of the century. Unfortunately, the church's promotion of this great need has subsided considerably since its membership consists no longer of immigrant laborers but of established middle-class workers. The need for unionization of workers is as great as ever, but the church seems to have lost heart. The meager committees that it sets up to aid migrant laborers and agricultural workers, for example, have little support from the church at large. Often the clerics working in labor, as well as lay workers, find that the established interests of the church offer the strongest resistance to social change.

The right to criticize, dissent, and protest for the purpose of social change must be vigorously defended by the church. In a time when even our own country is in danger of being dominated by the industrial feudalism of the industry-government-military complex, great forces of resistance will develop. The church, in its leadership role, must give weight and dignity to those forces in order to promote civil forms of expression. It is not a question of making the church relevant; the church is a human society that is always relevant. The question is to whom, to what interests is the church relevant, to all men or just to the interests of the managerial classes? To effectively declare the universality of salvation, it is imperative that the church be able to support a great diversity of social causes.

By a sort of gentleman's agreement, the church stays out of politics in this country. But the neutrality of the church is more apparent than real. Any neutrality or silence is a strong vote for the status quo. If the church is not interested in politics, politics is most interested in the church. It is time for the church to disenchant itself of its pretended neutrality, recognize that it is truly a participant in the growth of society, and begin to take responsibility for its political stands. Certainly the patronage of the wealthy will drop off whenever the church takes a stand in a controversial issue. But a church cannot have its prophets and its profits too. This is why it is so important for the church to be propertyless, so that it will have the mobility to do the nasty work of social protest when it is called for.

By the action of God in the life and teachings of Christ, the church has been planted in the middle of man's situation and has no option to reject its political role. It is a radically political organization.

Some people would have no objection to the church's activity in politics as long as it stays out of the realm of economics. Sure, let the church promote the cause of the poor and anybody else—as long as it does not affect the profits of certain businesses. The church has as much right as anybody else to enter politics, but no right to interfere with the free-wheeling laws of supply and demand. It has no competence in the field of business! We must answer to the contrary: the doctrine of the dignity of the individual has profound implications for the economic order. Money is not only a means to an end; in our society it is accepted as a measure of the worth of the individual. Since this is so, the church demands that wealth be distributed according to merit and talent, not according to social background, education, or chance. Money is needed for something more than to buy things, but to be somebody. Every person's voice in society must be endowed with the weight and dignity sufficient to demand respect. This means money. Unless each man is paid according to his relative worth, our whole creed of equal opportunity and human dignity is not worth the trouble of mouthing it.

Needless to say, such a Christian concept of an economic order demands great changes in American society. The great disparity in salaries and incomes between people who differ little in talent, industry, and dedication is criminal. The great number of hidden poor who are trapped in an economic short-circuit is an indictment of the injustices to be remedied. It is not to be expected, once these injustices are uncovered and diagnosed, that the American way of life can continue as before without incurring the sanctions of history. More and more the virtue and ethical self-satisfaction of the country will be challenged and questioned. The quality of the church's involvement in the social changes that must take place may well determine the continued existence of our country as a democracy. Unless the church can radically alter its economic posture, it will suffer the same punishments as others who cannot accept the demands of justice and social change.

How is the church to prepare its members for involvement in the progress of society? The first technique is that of religious education, to be taken up more fully in a following chapter. To develop qualities of independence and initiative in applying the doctrines of Christ to whatever situation the Christian finds himself in will demand forms of religious education far removed from the tribal indoctrination now taking place under Catholic auspices. The next technique is that of programmatic leadership: Catholics as groups directly espousing some social cause. It is my feeling that the parish itself should be the *smallest* unit of official political and social action. Catholics interested in causes not demanding parish action should be able to work independently in other groups. One qualification required upon entering the realms of social change is effectiveness. The fragmentation of official policy by splinter cell groups completely wastes needed strength. Catholics should refuse to do what they can within a restrictive situation and instead create pressure to involve the parish as a whole. If anything is worth doing by the parish as such, it demands parish involvement, not just the activity of a few peripheral groups. The first demand of social action is to guarantee the right of individuals and small groups to influence parish action. To forbid or restrict the interests of minority groups from becoming the interests of the whole parish is the most effective way of stopping the social mission of the church.

Such a policy would also prevent much confusion about who is speaking for the church. Every priest, nun, lay official, and social action group should be prevented from speaking for the church on social matters unless they are commissioned to do so by a well-determined consensus of the whole parish. If the parish is to take a stand on some important local issue, for example, any statement coming from the church should be voted on by the general membership. This is the only way that a new form of ecclesiastical imperialism by clerics and lay officials can be avoided. If a pastor wishes to bring the full resources of the church to bear on a situation, he must honestly admit that he is not his parish and that he must train and educate his resources so that they might take the desired action with him. Similarly, a bishop has no right to speak as the head of his church to the rest of the community without a well-founded consensus among his priests and people. He cannot take this for granted.

The best means of education for secular commitment is, of course, individual example. By seeing what other individuals are able to do in their situation, we have a point of reference by which we can judge ourselves and alter our values. This is where the personal witness of priests and nuns is most important. When one becomes a priest or nun, he does not lose his Christian obligation to love others. Rather, that obligation becomes intensified by reason of the more specialized dedication to religion. One is freed from the responsibilities of domestic life so that he may be more free, not less free, to serve God in the neighbor. The advantages of celibacy should allow clerics and religious to go and just raise Cain in the pursuit of justice. Their position of leadership within the Christian community obliges them to be exemplary in their secular involvement. The appearance of a strong lay leadership may be possible without clerical leadership. If the church wishes, priests can continue as prayer-leaders and administrators; professional lay leaders and organizers could be hired for the purpose of secular witness. But there are several problems in this solution. First of all, the clergy would have to step down from the position of leadership in what is the most important task of the church. Secondly, there is no theological justification for the dichotomy between the clergy and laymen in the matter of loving the neighbor. Love is directed toward *persons* in whatever need they experience; it cannot be directed to some needs but not to others. Finally, even if the clergy were reduced to performing the functions of Mass priests, they would still be obliged to give personal witness in the secular by reason of their status as baptized Christians. Whatever religious leadership is assumed by the laymen, the professional obligations of clerics and religious do not deprive them of the obligation of also getting involved in the secular: that's where God is.

There is a traditional as well as a scriptural justification for the secular involvement of priests and nuns. Their activity in teaching, charities, and hospitals directly related them to secular needs. The problem is that their involvement did not expand as the needs developed, probably the result of political pressures as well as institutional inertia. The freedom of certain religious communities to involve themselves in science and social work belongs by right to the individual parish as the basic action group of the church. The freedom to take part in community progress and controversy belongs by right to the priests and nuns as citizens and Christians.

There does remain a problem of identification of the role a priest plays when he takes a prominent part in social action: When is he acting as a private person and when as a spokesman for his congregation? This is an important distinction, but one which the individual priest can easily clarify. Usually it does not present much of a problem. A cleric can easily make public in whose name he is acting if there is a conflict or uncertainty of roles. Whether he is seen in a picket line or on a welfare planning council, it is assumed that he is acting out of personal conviction unless he states otherwise. It may be objected that a priest in a Roman collar is never acting as a private person, but always as a representative of the church. Certainly, we answer, the Roman collar endows the priest with a certain prestige as a leader of a Christian community, but it does not subordinate or eliminate his prestige as a citizen and a person. The professional commitment of judges, civil employees, teachers, and politicians does not absolve them from the responsibilities of citizenship, but only heightens them. The same holds true, especially true, of those whose lives are dedicated to the formation of conscience and responsibility. Their professional role cannot be exercised, in fact, without aggressive personal involvement in the secular community.

The freedom of the church and the freedom of secular society have a reciprocal effect on one another. Not only does God use the church to build up his kingdom in the world, but he uses secular society to develop the church. The church gets its cues about what it must be from its involvement in the historical situation in which it finds itself. The ethical development of mankind is not contained in some ideal pattern handed over to the church to be imposed upon the world. The ethical responsibilities of the church, and its own image of itself, change as man's needs and his control over his environment change. This is what we mean when we say that God speaks to his church through history. The church can only be as free as the society in which it lives. Likewise, secular society advances to the degree that the church can discern and support those elements of progress bearing the imprint of God's demand. The kingdom of God does not consist in brick and mortar but in humanizing the world.

CHAPTER FOUR

Race Is Grace

Ask not what the church can do for the Negro but what the Negro is doing to the church. There is much discussion about the support and resistance given by the church to the Negro revolt in America. The church's complicity in the development of institutional racism and its accomplishments in eliminating it are subjects of much debate. Modern prophets have fulminated against the church's silence; conservatives have condemned its participation in public demonstrations. Few have taken time to point out what is happening within the church itself as a result of the controversy, except to note the drop in membership where a pastor takes a strong stand or the sudden disappearance of a curate who takes a strong stand. Not too many people realize what is going on. The Negro is not asking for admission into our society; he is trying to lead a revolution to change our way of life. He is not satisfied with the rest of us and he aims to convert us. He knows that he will never be accepted into society with its present attitudes and social structure. He is out for big game—not just jobs, education, and housing. He is out to get *us*. He wants to radically change our accepted patterns of thought and behavior.

When the Negro comes pounding on our door demanding that we treat him like a person and nothing else, we have to admit that we have never treated *anybody* like a person and nothing else! The Negro claims that he plans to save us from ourselves, from those elements in our lives that keep *us* down: the political fallacies, the evasion and duplicity of our speech, the corruption in our business life, and the lack of simple decency in our everyday human dealings. The Negro feels that little democracy ever filters down to the man in the street. While we cherish the idea of democracy in government, we often submit ourselves to the worst forms of tyranny in education, employment, commerce, and community relations. If respect for human dignity is to be a reality in America, it must penetrate every institution that has a bearing on the common good. We pay lip service to justice for all as we salute the flag, and then we turn around and kick our neighbor in the crotch. The Negro knows that he is not the only one to suffer from this contradiction. The lack of equity of process in all areas of life puts us all at the short end of the freedom stick. The Negro is out to upset all of our institutions. This includes the churches.

First of all, the Negro has sparked a theological revolution. The churches of America have been unique in their development of a theology that supports both the theory and practice of racism. This development goes back to the days of the first plantation owners who imported African slaves. These planters were hardy and enterprising men who had inherited strong feelings about freedom and religion; they were the stock from which our great founders such as Thomas Jefferson would descend. Yet, in the harsh realities of the day, slavery seemed to be demanded by reason of economic necessity to protect the huge investments necessary for the development of the colonies.

If the planters were uneasy about the condition of their slaves, their Anglican pastors were more uneasy. Even if these black people were treated like animals at times, they surely must have *souls* to be saved. They were docile and intelligent. They seemed capable of accepting the truths necessary for baptism. At first the planters balked at the proposal to make Christians out of their slaves. They had certain social ideas about the implications of baptism. It makes men subjects of the Crown as well as members of the church, persons with rights and obligations entitled to self-determination and property ownership. Baptism means the benefits of civilization. That would not do.

A theological compromise was reached. The priests assured the planters that baptism does not affect the status of the ownership of one's body, only the soul. Baptism, would, in fact, make better slaves of them. Their souls would belong to Jesus, but their bodies would still belong to their masters. Salvation pertains only to the spiritual order of things, not the material order. After all, didn't Paul exhort slaves to be obedient to their owners? Intrigued with the idea of using religion as a means of social control, the planters gave the priests the go-ahead. But even as the waters of salvation began to flow, the slaves were required to take an oath stating that they were not requesting the Holy Spirit out of any plan to free themselves from the duty they owed their masters, but merely for the good of their souls and the grace promised to members of the church.

This oath set the pattern not only of the church's answer to slavery and segregation but also of its whole approach to the secular world of man. God is not relevant to the world. The only way we could afford to keep the Negro out of our society was by keeping God out of it. By making religion primarily a matter of rewards and punishments in the next world, we denied the reality and demands of this one. This life is but an artificial preparation for the world to come, the *real* world. The issues of the secular world became theatrical and unreal for the church. Spiritual realities are the only ones that count; the Negro has as much access to them, in his pitiable state, as anyone else.

The contribution of the Catholic Church to this theology was supported by its strong commitment to metaphysics. The legalism of the church demanded a great emphasis on the transcendence of God and the immateriality of salvation. In its theology of grace, it promoted the idea that man had to be divinized, made like God, before he could please God. Strict adherence to the regulations of the church were necessary in order to have access to sanctifying grace, a supernatural quality that somehow changed the substance of the spiritual soul. God's commitments to man's human condition were set aside; he had become man, not to aid man in developing his humanity, but to release him from it. Simply, men have to become something inhuman to be saved. They must escape their human condition before they are in a position of placating the demands of an unearthly God. The traditional scriptural doctrine of God's love for *this* world was replaced by a doctrine of God's love for a metaphysical subworld.

This theology was reinforced by the church's penitential discipline. The church in America inherited a European moral theology that refused to take seriously the moral autonomy of secular concerns. It offered grace and salvation to those who kept certain religious observances and avoided a rather limited number of categorized sins. This moral tradition was based on a conformity to written laws. But law itself is negative, telling people what they should not do, not what they are to do. A moral thinking dominated by legal conformity regards compliance with the restrictions of law as the fulfillment of God's ethical demands. There is the tendency to forget that the demands of justice are not met in the law and that the greatest range of our moral obligations remain beyond the law. As a result, Catholics took the catechism list of sins rather than the demands of conscience as the norm of morality. In matters of economic and social concerns, rarely touched upon in books and sermons, they suffered little restriction. Somehow, discrimination, social injustice, poor community relations, and lack of commercial ethics were never included in their lists of sins. The means of grace, namely, Mass and the sacraments, were available for everybody who desired them.

This was the church's contribution to the social order.

Recently, theologians have tried to deal more explicitly with the ethical concerns of the secular. But here again they have only expanded their categories of sins to include new restrictions and minimum obligations necessary for the granting of absolution in the sacrament of Penance. The moral tradition of the church is still dominated by a legalism that refuses to recognize the primacy of one's individual conscience and the resulting autonomy of secular commitment. In most local churches, morality is still defined in terms of religious acts and the avoidance of particular sins.

The Negro revolt has forced the church to recognize the authority of God in the secular developments of history. The church is coming to see that ethical progress does not originate with the pronouncements of its bishops and theologians. Somehow it is coming to accept the fact that God is the ethical leader of mankind and that he does not need the church for the building of his kingdom. God often uses the most secular of institutions to serve his purposes and the most unlikely and unreligious people to carry out his plans. The church is coming to see that there is really no need to take Christ into the market place; he is already there. The church is finally going to the market place to find Christ and to find itself. The Negro revolt is defining the church's own role in the world, not that of a master telling his pupils what to do, but of a servant who must learn from God's action in the world the demands it must carry out.

Finally, the church is learning that salvation means freedom, political, economic, academic, and social freedom. God's love for man is a full-bodied love that demands a full-bodied commitment of man to all of his brother's needs. A God who is not concerned with man's earthy needs is not the God proclaimed by Christ. If man is to please God, it is not by the possession of the sublife of metaphysical grace but by the ethical response to the needs of others. Goodness before God is not some superphysical perfection but moral development. The *one* thing required by God is love of the neighbor: house him, clothe him, give him a job, make him feel important in his community, treat him justly. The particular time, place, and circumstances of this response can never be spelled out by the church for every situation. All the church can do is point out the implications of the gospel for every situation of life and rely on the Holy Spirit to direct each man in the application of the gospel to his own concrete situation. The Negro revolt is bringing the church to recognize that the source of its own authority is not found in some metaphysical formulae but in the authority of each man's conscience.

The Negro revolt is also bringing the church to correct its great structural weaknesses. The many failures of the church to provide effective leadership to the revolution going on demonstrates the immobility of its organization. This failure has been most evident where the church finally decided to become involved and test its strength in the racial conflict. The campaign of the churches to defeat Proposition 14 in California in 1964, which outlaws any form of fair-housing laws, was so badly organized and ineffective that few people were aware of the churches' stand. Earlier in 1963, the quality of ecclesiastical leadership was exposed in the National Conference on Race and Religion in Chicago. This conference had been organized by the top-level administrators of our Catholic, Protestant, and Jewish faiths. One perceptive commentator described the event in the following manner:

> The Conference was so out of touch with the realities of the racial revolt in America, that, in the main, it failed to recognize or address them. . . . Another indication of the massive indifference to and ignorance of the intensity, pathology, and alienation represented by the racial crisis was the manner in which the Negroes were treated in the Conference leadership itself. Apart from the single exception of Martin Luther King, no Negro

spokesman was on the program of the Conference, except for those who introduced other speakers, entertained the delegates, or prayed over the deliberations. Uncle Tom was the most popular Negro at the National Conference on Religion and Race. His days are gone forever, engulfed in the tides of the revolution the nation now suffers. But it is important to remember that one of his last days was spent at this Conference of the churches of the land, saying, "yes, suh," to the most banal clichés within the vocabulary of the white religionists, praising the "progress" that has been achieved in race relations in America within the very shadow of Chicago's teeming black ghettos, and reciting in unison the sentimental psalms of interfaith meetings about the fatherhood of God and the brotherhood of men (William Stringfellow, *My People Is the Enemy*. New York: Holt, Rinehart and Winston, Inc., 1964; 150 pp. Pp. 135–136.).

The church cannot contribute to the development of secular society without undergoing development itself. It will remain a drag on the progress of democracy until it becomes more democratic. The failure of the church to give effective ethical leadership in the racial struggle of America is representative of its performance in similar situations throughout the world. It is not a question of whether the church is exercising effective leadership. Its great size and power make its leadership extremely effective. But effective for what? It would not be so bad if the church merely chose to neutralize its political power, as some American bishops think they are doing; but leadership is never neutral, power is always being employed, for good or ill. And the most effective type of leadership is silence about truth, especially the truth about injustice. The failure of the church to raise a strong cry against racism in Europe and America perpetrated one of the greatest crimes against humanity committed in the name of religion. Never has cowardice in leadership been more destructive.

Ethical leadership is impossible with the unethical political structures within the church. How can the church effectively combat the restrictive paternalism that oppresses the Negro in secular society as long as it remains the most paternalistic of all societies? In every organization and group there are two forms of leadership, the official leadership and the real or prophetical leadership. In a group discussion, for example, there are usually found the moderator, who is usually appointed to direct the discussion; and one participant, who contributes most of the insights to the discussion. A successful discussion often depends upon a good working relationship between the official leader and the real leader. If they work together, they are able to evoke a maximum of participation and insight from the rest of the group. The same is true for organizations of larger sizes. Communications must be kept open at all times for the dialogue to develop between the official leaders and the real prophets of the church. Presently, the structures of the church are designed to prevent such dialogue from taking place. As a result, the official leadership aligns itself with commercial and political interests outside the church rather than the prophetical leadership within it.

The Bible teaches that every man is endowed with a certain amount of prophetical inspiration. The task of the church must be to reorganize its structures and procedures so that each believer can properly make his contribution to the prophetical leadership of the church. Insofar as any person is prevented from making his contribution to the church's life, the doctrine of God's presence with man is denied. But insofar as reformed organizational patterns of the church reflect the work and power of God in every individual, they will serve not only the cause of the American Negro, but of all men. The church must become ethical in order to serve the needs of secular society.

The church bears a *public* responsibility to reorganize immediately its structural patterns according to responsible and accepted standards. The American Negro is in a position to bring about this reorganization. He is on the short end of the freedom stick in the church now. The lack of equity of process within the church militates against the Negro's full participation as a Catholic. His civil rights are often violated as well as his religious rights. Whenever he is refused a seat in a Catholic school, a job as a teacher, admittance to a seminary, or a seat in church, he is left no recourse within the church. Whenever a priest or religious is silenced or mysteriously transferred because of promoting integration, secular society as well as the church suffers from such arbitrary action. It does not take much investigation to reveal that the refusal to submit to due process within the church destroys communication and leadership in every area of church life. But it took the Negro revolt to bring this to light. The American Negro is the tracer dye that reveals the serious inequities in the church as well as in the rest of society.

We can hardly expect the church to give much leadership to the Negro revolt before new legal guarantees are worked into church law that would protect the civil and ecclesiastical rights of all church members. Such a reform would necessarily include the abolition of such malicious and anachronistic laws such as Canons 120, 2334, and 2341, which prohibit legal action against clerics and bishops, and Canon 2222, which allows disciplinary action to be taken against clerics without due process. The star-chamber proceedings that take place in our chancery offices should be quickly eliminated before they are declared unconstitutional by the American courts. The argument that the church is incompatible with the beliefs of a free society can be proved by pointing to these vicious laws. They not only deprive the Negro and white Catholics of some of their most important civil rights; they educate them, not for responsibility in democracy, but for subservience in tyranny.

Joseph R. Washington, Jr. briefly touched upon the social difficulties facing the Negro in the church in his work

Black Religion, The Negro and Christianity in the United States (Boston: Beacon Press, 1964; 306 pp.):

> A clear signal of the progress of Roman Catholicism among Negroes will be the promotion of Negroes to positions of prestige beyond the local church and over white and colored Catholics (P. 244.).
>
> Whether or not the emerging importance of laymen will affect the Roman Catholic encounter with the Negro remains in the speculative state (P. 245.).
>
> In the North, Roman Catholic compartmentalization takes the form of white priests, teachers, and administrators in authority over Negro persons. Catholics have not taken seriously the full inclusion of Negroes on every level, and have tended to be concerned about social problems which have captured the imagination of the Negro. In the long run, Negroes will not be satisfied with an approach which tends to do things for them instead of with them. A deliberate and sustained effort to accept Negroes in strategic places will be necessary if they are to be recruited for the mission of the church. Without substantial endeavor at the point of equal participation, Roman Catholics may be able to make capital of the Negro's drive for desegregation and against discrimination, but its Negro members will be largely dead weight (P. 247.).

One of the greatest demands of the Negro revolt is church reform. We must ask what changes in the procedures governing the placement of bishops and pastors will be necessary to provide Washington's suggested token representation of minority groups in every level of church government. It is not enough to appoint Negro priests to serve Negro congregations or to consecrate African bishops to serve only in Africa. With a structure that reserves the control of the Roman Curia to Italians and the local diocesan curia to white business men, what chance has the American Negro to participate fully in the life of the church? Commitment to racial justice demands much more than canonizing dead Negroes; it demands full attention to all the needs of live ones. Until we are ready to entrust our black brothers with the administration of the church, our sincerity is suspect when we speak about the universality of salvation. Justice demands the presence of Negroes in the official leadership of the church.

The prophetical leadership within the church must be given strong guarantees for freedom of speech in *all* areas and situations, not just in places where race has become a respectable issue. Until now, most of the noise seems to be coming from where the greatest racial activity, not the greatest need, is. This gives the false impression that the social doctrines are being enforced in other areas as well. But examination would show that the racial activity of the church in such areas as Chicago and St. Louis is *not the same* as in most other areas and *is the same* as in other institutions operating in those two cities. This indicates that the church is merely following the policy of the local situation, whatever it happens to be. In most central urban areas with a high concentration of Negroes, business, labor, and government are also very active in promoting racial justice; it would be a shock indeed if the church were not also involved.

Often the church in those areas is credited with not leaving with the whites, as many of the white Protestant churches did at the time of the transition. Is this to be attributed to the enlightened leadership of the Catholics? This could hardly be the case in view of the inability of pastors to prevent the whites from moving out in the first place. The maintenance of parishes in areas that often change from a strongly Catholic area to a low Catholic population is due to an ancient policy of the Roman Church of never relinquishing any property it has once gained. The Roman Church regards its property as a private and sacred inheritance, never to be alienated. Because of this policy, it takes an act of the Roman Curia to abolish a parish or to sell any property worth more than five thousand dollars (Canon 1532, 1). If the church happens to be in an all-Negro area, it usually is because there happened to be a white congregation there in the first place; as usual, the Negroes inherit the leftovers that the whites could not take with them to the suburbs.

Similar problems arise because of the church's rigorous legislation on parish boundaries and the jurisdiction of the pastor. The inflexibility of the boundaries is often used as a tool of segregation. The lack of inter-parish programs and co-operation limits and divides the exercise of effective leadership in controversial issues. Both pastors and people can hide behind the shield of legal regulations to avoid seeing what is going on all around them.

Besides the legal obstacles within the church to the Negro revolt, there is positive financial resistance. The church is just beginning to wake up to the social responsibilities inherent in its economic power. It was formerly assumed that money was indifferent to the ethical development of society as long as the terms of contracts were fulfilled. The church felt it could freely operate in the arena of business and commerce with a certain amount of neutrality and immunity from implication in social issues. Ever anxious to prove its compatibility with the American way of life, the church gave birth to a whole generation of organization clerics to manage its commercial affairs. The church is big business, yearly negotiating millions of dollars in services, building contracts, investments, and supplies. But we have yet to learn that business is a part of the ethical world in which we live and is not indifferent to the needs of just social patterns and relationships.

Money has the power of directing social patterns. Every contract and purchase is fraught with social meaning and purpose. We cannot spend a dime without building up or tearing down the kingdom of God; money brings tremendous social responsibilities. Business done with banks that withhold funds from integrated housing projects, doing business with discriminatory building contractors, accepting advertising from firms engaged in unfair employment practices, and dealing with interests promoting racist housing patterns are a few of the ways in which the church attacks the kingdom of God.

The church is a tax-exempt public institution. Its financial negotiations are a matter of public concern and are therefore a matter of public record. The former practice of not letting even Catholics review the fiscal policies of the church indicated the possible commitment of the church to outside interests. The recent introduction of nondiscrimination clauses in the contracts negotiated by a few dioceses may indicate a new era of public responsibility in the church. The lack of public regulation of church expenditures is a formidable obstacle to social justice.

The drive of the Negro for equality will perhaps bring significant changes in the educational framework of the church. Many church people are coming to realize that, in a matter of social concern, the church cannot just tell people what to think and then expect immediate conformity. There are too many vested interests and ingrained patterns of thought connected with social injustice to make it merely a matter of telling. Religious education and the teaching of the social doctrine of the church demand the use of persuasion and training. There are many other institutions and voices bidding for the attention of citizens in today's world. If the church is to be effective, it must give witness in a way that is dramatic, effective, and, most of all, respectful of people's intelligence. Educational competence, and not just peremptory dictation on what is right and wrong, is indispensable in the field of race relations.

Race relations is basically human relations, a field that demands the best methods of adult educational procedures. At present the Catholic Church is most weak in the field of adult education; its educational system is basically child-centered. It has been known for some time that changes in racial attitudes take place in adulthood, not childhood, where they are faithfully copied from parents. The teaching of abstract moral principles in church and school has little effect on the racial attitudes of children. Even appeals made to religious motivation have little effect on them. Until children reach adolescence, the will of God for them is what their parents demand and feel. The service rendered the God of religion class is but a game in comparison to the worship given to the gods of hearth and home. Even people who accept a God of love are able to promote and defend segregation as his will.

Sermons also are poor educational means for changing racial attitudes. Study groups and discussions on the racial doctrine of the church are helpful for those already committed, but they too can be harmful by leaving the impression that social matters can be so easily solved by such an academic approach. Effective action and social commitment do not arise from knowing where the church stands on an issue. The reduction of prejudice, as any other change in basic attitudes, comes only with personal involvement in the situation. We learn new attitudes by relating in new ways to people. New relationships give us new points of reference by which we can judge and evaluate our own attitudes. Education in basic matters of life depends upon this interpersonal interaction.

Vicarious identification with victims of prejudice is one form of involving oneself in a new situation. Listening to or reading a story about what happens to real people is a much better way of changing attitudes than the teaching of abstract principles. Stories force the listener to defend what he would have done in the same situation. For this reason, books on social protest are needed in religious education. In reading and discussing the works of W. E. B. DuBois, James Baldwin, John Howard Griffin, Richard Wright, and Louis Lomax, students can often identify with the victims of prejudice and appreciate values never encountered before. There is also a need for the introduction into our history textbooks of the contributions of Negroes and members of other minority groups to civilization.

Another method of prejudice reduction is the human relations course. This usually involves a scientific examination of racial stereotype attitudes and the common fallacies connected with them, discussions on Negro history, local and national problems of segregation, and the nature and work of the civil rights groups. This type of course is most helpful for priests, teachers, administrators, counselors, policemen, and personnel managers. Human relations TV institutes for teachers can be developed to give widest possible coverage to whole school districts. It cannot be presumed that the teacher will automatically drop his white middle-class values upon entering a class of minority groups. Unless he is given adequate instruction in the values of other cultures, his negative reactions to the students will only alienate them further from the school situation.

It has been shown in various studies that human relations courses are not effective unless they are conducted by competent instructors over a period of twenty or thirty weeks. It is not likely that many Catholic institutions could afford to present such a rigorous course, but they are able to promote and support its presentation in co-operation with other local institutions. Needless to remark, the more need there is for such a course, the more is opposition encountered in presenting it. Often local university extension services are willing to accept invitations to conduct such courses. While these are usually presented for the benefit of teachers, they are often open to the public.

The success of interracial councils and interracial home visits—in which different groups can meet for the purposes of developing better relations between them—depends largely on the support given such activities by the community at large. The artificiality of coming together merely to meet members of other groups rarely develops into communication on meaningful levels that would change attitudes. Usually people participating in such activities are committed to begin with. Human relations councils can have an important role to play with the rest of the community, however, as a pressure group. The effectiveness of the Los Angeles County Commission on Human Relations in anticipating and resolving interracial needs depends largely on the support it gives to the development of local human relations groups. Such community-based councils avoid some of the criticism of being outside agitators not knowing the local problems. But if they are to induce change, they must feel free to enter politics, take public stands, and create pressure strong enough to be effective—usually through the use of the local press and the open forums of the city council and the meetings of other organizations.

Rabbi Henry Cohen, in an article, "Prejudice Reduction in Religious Education" (*Religious Education* [New York], Vol. LIX, No. 5, P. 390), summarizes a number of studies on the effectiveness of different techniques and approaches to the problem of changing racial attitudes. He states: "Empirical studies have tended to emphasize three conditions which have been found to encourage prejudice reduction when they occur together: 1) equal status contact of groups, 2) in pursuit of common (superordinate) goals, 3) in a situation in which intergroup friendship has community support." He emphasizes that there should be opportunity for *social* contacts between the members of different groups. They need common projects to work on, goals which are superordinate to their need to know one another better. Working together, members of the differing groups will naturally and freely exchange information about themselves and education will take place. If there is community support for the friendships that develop through such contacts, the resulting change in racial attitudes may be lasting. The obvious problem in this formula is the development of public support for interracial friendships.

Rabbi Cohen remarks that the existing methods and framework of religious education are not at all geared to the task of prejudice reduction, which involves, as it does, social action and community support. He does suggest the use of summer camps and youth councils as a feasible means of implementing the above formula. Interracial and interfaith groups in which leaders create a mystique that supports acceptance and diversity could take up worthwhile community projects in which friendships would develop. But the parochial limitations on programs of religious education militate against such contacts. The churches are often the strongest defenders of both religious and racial separation. In the problem of prejudice reduction, we have a clear example of the church's ability to teach injustice. Religious education turns out to be antireligious education. Can religious education be Christian?

If the church is to fulfill its task of pointing out the presence of God's kingdom in the world, it will have to disown its institutional insecurity and direct its efforts to the promotion of justice. The best form of education consists in action, especially in matters of human relations. The demands of the gospel are not imparted through a systematized defense of religious practices—which most of Catholic religious education is—but only in the works of justice. The failure of the church in race is, in the simplest analysis, a failure to teach and practice justice—the concern for the basic needs of others. What keeps the Negro down are the violations of justice as made known in conscience. If the church is to offer the Negro revolt any more than token support, it must stop telling people that men are brothers. It must start acting as if it believed that God himself is our brother, one not to be found just in the sanctuary and catechism class, but out there in the world where people are helping people. If someone were to ask

Christ today where the kingdom of God can be found, I believe he would say in the civil rights groups, student protests, in the picket lines, the settlement houses, remedial reading programs, tutorial projects, welfare planning councils, youth rehabilitation and job training, child study centers for retarded and mentally disturbed children, medical and mental health clinics, assistance leagues, congressional reapportionment, voter registration, English and citizenship classes, political-party volunteer work, union organization and labor legislation, low-rent housing, integrated schools, low classroom loads, interfaith meetings and celebrations, and in the reunion of the churches—in short, in everything the Negro stands for in his drive for equality.

CHAPTER FIVE

Getting Ready

The only trouble with Christian education today is that it attempts to teach people about God. If you ask any child or adult why they go to religion class, the answer will be, "To learn about God." The churches of America spend millions of dollars yearly developing and carrying out religious education programs in the sincere conviction that the modern techniques of education bring people to the knowledge of God. Catholics have firmly committed themselves to the operation of a separate school system in order to carry out the most elaborate program of religious education conceived in the history of the church. Adult religious education has been evaluated, strengthened, and given a new lease on life as a means of making God more understandable to the inquiring mind. The stepped-up educational concerns of our society at large have been matched within the church by directing more and more of the church's resources to the service of a doctrinal approach to God. In all of this, there stands out the almost universal acceptance of the idea that God can be apprehended in the religion class.

Religious education is a major concern of the church, perhaps *the* major concern. And no one questions the value and importance of education, psychiatry, and the social sciences in religious pedagogy. But we should question whether the purpose of religious education is to teach people about *God*. The bulk of our theology teaches that God is attainable only through faith, an act that is primarily dependent upon the free intervention of God in the life of the individual. There is sufficient evidence to believe that God is completely unteachable; he resists being analyzed, explained, defined, or reduced to doctrinal propositions. He has given us no assurance that he will submit himself to a lesson plan or the curricula of religious education. The first task of Christian education, it would seem, is to proclaim that it does not attempt to teach about God. The last thing Christian education can afford to be is religious.

We can teach *things*. But we can't teach people. We can teach *about* people, but even here problems arise. Learning about people, as satisfying as it might be, is never the same as knowing them. The relationship we have with people merely by learning about them is a very tenuous and often superficial one. We really don't know a person unless we commit ourselves to his needs, ambitions, and desires. Love is the only human manner of knowing persons. This is even more true of God. God is too much a person to be learned about. He can only be met, confronted, addressed, and answered. Because God is so personable, there is nothing other people can tell us about him. The only knowledge we can have of God is that of a radical obedience to his desires and purposes. The knowledge of God is fundamentally intellectual, but it is something much more than that. It demands a full commitment of one's drives and powers; the knowledge of God is attained in the exercise of the will. It does not consist in theories, answers, or formulae but in decisions and conduct. It does not rest in the intellectual sphere of life but in the moral and ethical one. God is known only in doing his will. For this reason, nothing that anybody says about God brings us in contact with God. We find God only by waiting for his demand in our personal and social lives and then submitting to it. God is met in the ethical decisions of life, in seeking and doing his will as made known to us by prophetic men and our own conscience.

The ethical context of Christianity radically binds it to the interpersonal, cultural, and historical development of men. Because God is known in the demands of conscience, it follows that the patterns of history reveal the purposes and plan of God. History does not consist in a series of mechanical happenings chronologically recorded, but in the free decisions of men responding to ethical demands. Cultures are not created simply by the physical environments and limitations of men, but by their free and unpredictable response to their situations. God speaks to men primarily not through physical nature but through their interpersonal relationships. Men were able to attain the conception of God as creator of the universe only after they had discovered God's activity as the Lord of peoples and nations, of families and individuals. The people of Israel were led from the recognition of God's control of history to the belief in his work of creation, and not the other way around. The creation of nature, the theater of human history, is merely a part of that history. The living God of the Bible is the God of men first of all and the God of nature secondly. For Christians, man is the measure of all things, even of his knowledge of God. The knowledge of God and the service of man are not to be identified, but it is in the service of man that the knowledge of God is attained.

The knowledge of God, as attained in loving the neighbor, is of the very essence of Christian faith. It is not a condition required for obtaining some other good—grace, merit, or a mystical or metaphysical participation in God's nature. The obediential love of God is in itself its own reward, God's greatest gift to man, the result of the operation of his spirit in the world. The centrality of man's ethical concerns in his religious development is perhaps the most dominant and consistent theme we find in the Bible. A few quotes serve to show that religion is basically ethical. Even in the Old Testament, this teaching clearly emerges.

EXODUS 20:5–6. "For I, the LORD, your God, am a jealous God, inflicting punishment for their father's wickedness on the children of those who hate me, down to the third and fourth generations; but bestowing mercy down to the thousandth generation, on the children of those who love me and keep my commandments."

DEUTERONOMY 4:39–40. "This is why you must now know, and fix in your heart, that the LORD is God in the heavens and on earth below, and that there is no other. You must keep his statutes and commandments which I enjoin on you today, that you and your children after you may prosper, and that you may have long life on the land which the LORD, your God, is giving you forever."

DEUTERONOMY 6:4–7. "Hear, O Israel! The LORD is our God, the LORD alone! Therefore, you shall love the LORD, your God, with all your heart, and with all your soul, and with all your strength. Take to heart these words which I enjoin on you today. Drill them into your children. Speak of them at home and abroad, whether you are busy or at rest."

DEUTERONOMY 10:12–14. "And now, Israel, what does the LORD, your God, ask of you but to fear the LORD, your God, and follow his ways exactly, to love and serve the LORD, your God, with all your heart and all your soul, to keep the commandments and statutes of the LORD, which I enjoin on you today for your own good?"

DEUTERONOMY 30:11–14. "For this command which I enjoin on you today is not too mysterious and remote for you. It is not up in the sky, that you should say, 'Who will go up in the sky to get it for us and tell us of it, that we may carry it out?' Nor is it across the sea, that you should say, 'Who will cross the sea to get it for us and tell us of it, that we may carry it out?' No, it is something very near to you, already in your mouths and in your hearts; you have only to carry it out."

PSALMS 111:9, 10. He has sent deliverance to his people;
he has ratified his covenant forever; holy and awesome is his name.
The fear of the LORD is the beginning of wisdom;
prudent are all who live by it.

PROVERBS 1:7. The fear of the LORD is the beginning of knowledge;
wisdom and instruction fools despise.

PROVERBS 9:10. The beginning of wisdom is the fear of the LORD,
and knowledge of the Holy One is understanding.

SIRACH 1:16–18. Wisdom's garland is fear of the LORD,
with blossoms of peace and perfect health.
Knowledge and full understanding she showers down;
she heightens the glory of those who possess her.
The root of wisdom is fear of the LORD;
her branches are length of days.

JEREMIAH 22:15–16. Did not your father eat and drink?
He did what was right and just,
and it went well with him.
Because he dispensed justice to the weak and poor,
it went well with him.
Is this not true knowledge of me?
says the LORD.

HOSEA 6:6. For it is love that I desire, not sacrifice,
and knowledge of God rather than holocausts.

The Old Testament sets the stage for Christ by putting man's salvation in the realm of ethics—man's love of God and obedience to his demand. The experience of the prophets' encounter with God was to be extended to all of mankind. God's election of Israel, and especially of the men he had chosen to speak to Israel, was the pattern of the whole world's salvation. God's intervention in the history of men to invite them to share in his enterprise of building his kingdom on earth was to be accomplished in the practical business of everyday living, of social relationships, and current events. G. Ernest Wright, American Biblical scholar, describes the concreteness of our life with God in the following terms:

The experience of God conveyed no complete theology, no statement of abstract doctrines, no precious feelings that were cherished for years hence. The experience was too awful to be sentimentalized, to be made either pretty or petty. It was rather God's way of turning a man around in his tracks and confronting him with his job. "Here is the way! Walk in it!" "Here is your work. Go, do it!"

It is clear that the knowledge of God gained through these experiences was not a static faith floating through a man's consciousness; it was something to be done. Knowledge and truth in the Bible involve things to do, not simply a belief in a God of nature nor an experience of the God within. God is too busy, too active, too dynamic to wait for us to experience him in the acts of worship we devise in our schedules. He is to be known by what he has done and said, by what he is now doing and saying; and he is known when we do what he commands us to do (G. Ernest Wright and Reginald H. Fuller, *The Book of the Acts of God.* Garden City, N.Y.: Doubleday & Co., Inc., 1960; 420 pp. P. 22.).

Knowledge, then, is not of God's eternal being but of his claim upon us. It is the reverent acknowledgment of God's power, of his grace and requirement. Hence knowledge is not a private, inner possession of the knower. Man has knowledge only when he obeys, only when he acts in obedience. Knowledge involves the movement of the *will,* so that *not to know* is an error not correctable by more good ideas; it is a *guilt,* a rebellion. He who knows God is he who reverently acknowledges God's power and God's claim, a claim which leads him to practice brotherly love, justice, and righteousness (P. 24.).

Christ came, not to replace the centrality of ethical concerns in religion, but to verify it, once and for all. He did this first of all by developing men's concept of God as one who is loving and forgiving. God's free initiative in loving man is the basis for man's love of God and his neighbor. Christ's person and his mission, especially as operating in his death and resurrection, is primarily the declaration of God's ethical concern for man. This is the great secret and mystery to be proclaimed by the church also: God loves man. Secondly, Christ clearly distinguished between the law of God and the law of man, especially as operative in the Law of Moses. He emphasized that the root of human law is the will of God as made manifest in conscience. Christ firmly established the primacy of conscience as over and against, as well as within, all human law, whether civil, ecclesiastical, or domestic. It is conscience that gives force to human law; it is conscience that sits in judgment on human law. Thirdly, Christ offered himself as an example of true human obedience to God's will in the service of his neighbor. In the divine economy of Christianity, what served to declare God's goodness also serves the welfare of men and vice versa. Christ came to declare God's goodness by dying in defense of the dignity of the human person. From his time on, whatever serves man's need and dignity reveals the goodness of God. A few quotes will serve to show the priority of ethical, not intellectual or mystical, concerns in the New Testament religion.

1. God's love for man is declared in Christ:

LUKE 12:27–31. "Consider how the lilies grow; they neither toil nor spin, yet I say to you that not even Solomon in all his glory was arrayed like one of these. But if God so clothes the grass which flourishes in the field today but tomorrow is thrown into the oven, how much more you, O you of little faith!

"And as for you, do not seek what you shall eat, or what you shall drink; and do not exalt yourselves (for after all these things the nations of the world seek); but your Father knows that you need these things. But seek the kingdom of God, and all these things shall be given you besides. Do not be afraid, little flock, for it has pleased your Father to give you the kingdom."

LUKE 11:10–13. "For everyone who asks receives; and he who seeks finds; and to him who knocks it shall be opened. But if one of you asks his father for a loaf, will he hand him a stone? or for a fish, will he for a fish hand him a serpent? or if he asks for an egg, will he hand him a scorpion? Therefore, if you, evil as you are, know how to give good gifts to your children, how much more will your heavenly Father give the Good Spirit to those who ask him!"

LUKE 15:1–4, 7. Now the publicans and sinners were drawing near to him to listen to him. And the Pharisees and the Scribes murmured, saying, "This man welcomes sinners and eats with them."

But he spoke to them this parable, saying, "What man of you having a hundred sheep, and losing one of them, does not leave the ninety-nine in the desert, and go after that which is lost, until he finds it? I say to you that, even so, there will be joy in heaven over one sinner who repents, more than over ninety-nine just who have no need of repentance."

JOHN 3:16–17. For God so loved the world that he gave his only begotten Son, that those who believe in him may not perish, but may have life everlasting. For God did not send his Son into the world in order to judge the world, but that the world might be saved through him.

ROMANS 5:8. But God commends his charity towards us, because when as yet we were sinners, Christ died for us.

ROMANS 8:38–39. For I am sure that neither death, nor life, nor angels, nor principalities, nor things present, nor things to come, nor powers, nor height, nor depth, nor any other creature will be able to separate us from the love of God, which is in Christ Jesus our Lord.

II CORINTHIANS 5:17–19. If then any man is in Christ, he is a new creature: the former things have passed away; behold, they are made new! But all things are from God, who has reconciled us to himself through Christ and has given to us the ministry of reconciliation.

For God was truly in Christ, reconciling the world to himself by not reckoning against men their sins and by entrusting to us the message of reconciliation.

I JOHN 4:9–10. In this has the love of God been shown in our case, that God has sent his only-begotten Son into the world that we may live through him. In this is the love, not that we have loved God, but that he has first loved us, and sent his Son a propitiation for our sins.

2. Man's fellowship with God is moral in nature:

MATTHEW 5:43–48. "You have heard that it was said, 'Thou shalt love thy neighbor, and shalt hate thy enemy.' But I say to you, love your enemies, do good to those who hate you, and pray for those who persecute and calumniate you, so that you may be children of your Father in heaven, who makes his sun to rise on the good and the evil, and sends rain on the just and the unjust. For if you love those that love you, what reward shall you have? Do not even the publicans do that? And if you salute your brethren only, what are you doing more than others? Do not even the Gentiles do that?

"You therefore are to be perfect, even as your heavenly Father is perfect."

MATTHEW 7:21–23. "Not everyone who says to me 'Lord, Lord,' shall enter the kingdom of heaven; but he who does the will of my Father in heaven shall enter the kingdom of heaven. Many will say to me in that day, 'Lord, Lord, did we not prophesy in thy name, and cast out devils in thy name, and work many miracles in thy name?' And then I will declare to them, 'I never knew you. Depart from me, you workers of iniquity!'"

MATTHEW 10:24–25, 34–39. "No disciple is above his teacher, nor is the servant above his master. It is enough for the disciple to be like his teacher, and for the servant to be like his master. If they have called the master of the house Beelzebub, how much more those of his household!

"Do not think that I have come to send peace upon the earth; I have come to bring a sword, not peace. For I have come to set a man at variance with his father, and a daughter with her mother, and a daughter-in-law with her mother-in-law; and a man's enemies will be those of his own household. He who loves father or mother more than me is not worthy of me; and he who loves son or daughter more than me is not worthy of me. And he who does not take up his cross and follow me, is not worthy of me. He who finds his life will lose it, and he who loses his life for my sake, will find it."

MATTHEW 12:47–50. And someone said to him, "Behold thy mother and thy brethren are standing outside, seeking thee." But he answered and said to him who told him, "Who is my mother and who are my brethren?" And stretching forth his hand towards his disciples, he said, "Behold my mother and my brethren! For whoever does the will of my Father in heaven, is my brother and sister and mother."

MATTHEW 16:26–28. "For what does it profit a man, if he gain the whole world, but suffer the loss of his own soul? For the Son of Man is to come with his angels in the glory of his Father, and then he will render to everyone according to his conduct."

MARK 7:8–9, 13–16. "For, letting go the commandment of God, you hold fast the tradition of men, the washing of pots and cups; and many other things you do like to these."

And he said to them, "Well do you nullify the commandment of God, that you may keep your own tradition! You make void the commandment of God by your tradition, which you have handed down, and many suchlike things you do."

Then he called the crowd to him again, and said to them, "Hear me, all of you, and understand. There is nothing outside a man that, entering into him, that can defile him; but the things that come out of a man, these are what defile a man. If anyone has ears to hear, let him hear."

LUKE 11:27–28. Now it came to pass as he was saying these things, that a certain woman from the crowd lifted up her voice and said to him, "Blessed is the womb that bore thee, and the breasts that nursed thee." But he said, "Rather, blessed are they who hear the word of God and keep it."

LUKE 17:20–21. And on being asked by the Pharisees, "When is the kingdom of God coming?" he answered and said to them, "The kingdom of God comes unawares. Neither will they say, 'Behold, here it is,' or 'Behold, there it is.' For behold, the kingdom of God is within you."

JOHN 13:12–17. Now after he had washed their feet and put on his garments, when he had reclined again, he said to them, "Do you know what I have done to you? You call me Master and Lord, and you say well, for so I am. If therefore, I the Lord and Master have washed your feet, you also ought to wash the feet of one another. For I have given you an example, that as I have done to you, so you also should do. Amen, Amen, I say to you, no servant is greater than his master, nor is one who is sent greater than he who sent him.

JOHN 15:9–17. "As the Father has loved me, I also have loved you. Abide in my love. If you keep my commandments you will abide in my love, as I also have kept my Father's commandments, and abide in his love. These things I have spoken to you that your joy may be full.

"This is my commandment, that you love one another as I have loved you. Greater love than this no man has, that one lay down his life for his friends. You are my friends if you do the things I command you. No longer do I call you servants, because the servant does not know what his master does. But I have called you friends, because all things that I have heard from my Father I have made known to you. You have not chosen me, but I have chosen you, and have appointed you that you should go and bear fruit, and that your fruit should remain; that whatever you ask the Father in my name he may give you. These things I command you, that you may love one another."

I PETER 1:14–16, 22. As obedient children, do not conform to the lusts of former days when you were ignorant; but as the One who called you is holy, be you also holy in all your behavior; for it is written, "You shall be holy, because I am holy." Now that your obedience to charity has purified your souls for a brotherly love that is sincere, love one another heartily and intensely.

I PETER 3:13–18. And who is to harm you, if you are zealous for what is good? But even if you suffer anything for justice' sake, blessed are you. So have no fear of their fear and do not be troubled. But hallow the Lord Christ in your hearts. Be ready always with an answer to everyone who asks a reason for the hope that is in you. Yet do so with gentleness and fear, having a good conscience, so that wherein they speak in disparagement of you they who revile your good behavior in Christ may be put to shame. For it is better, if the will of God should so will, that you suffer for doing good than for doing evil. Because Christ also died once for sins, the Just for the unjust, that he might bring us to God.

I JOHN 3:16–18. In this we have come to know his love, that he laid down his life for us; and we likewise ought to lay down our life for the brethren. He who has the goods of this world and sees his brother in need and closes his heart to him, how does the love of God abide in him? My dear children, let us not love in word, neither with the tongue, but in deed and in truth.

3. Finally, it is Christ's obedience to God that accomplishes man's salvation. Man shares in that salvation by participating in Christ's obedience:

LUKE 2:49. "Did you not know that I must be about my Father's business?"

JOHN 4:34–35. Jesus said to them, "My food is to do the will of him who sent me, to accomplish his work. Do you not say, 'There are yet four months, and then comes the harvest'? Well, I say to you, lift up your eyes and behold that the fields are already white for the harvest."

JOHN 5:17–19. Jesus, however, answered them, "My Father works even until now, and I work." This, then, is why the Jews were the more anxious to put him to death; because he not only broke the Sabbath, but also called God his own Father, making himself equal to God. In answer therefore Jesus said to them, "Amen, amen, I say to you, the Son can do nothing of himself, but only what he sees the Father doing. For whatever he does, this the Son also does in like manner."

JOHN 6:38–39. "For I have come down from heaven, not to do my own will, but the will of him who sent me. Now this is the will of him who sent me, the Father, that I should lose nothing of what he has given me, but that I should raise it up on the last day."

JOHN 8:28–29. "When you have lifted up the Son of Man, then you will know that I am he, and that of myself I do nothing: but that I preach only what the Father has taught me. And he who sent me is with me; he has not left me alone, because I do always the things that are pleasing to him."

JOHN 10:17–18. "For this reason the Father loves me, because I lay down my life that I may take it up again. No one takes it from me, but I lay it down of myself. I have the power to lay it down, and I have the power to take it up again. Such is the command I have received from my Father."

MARK 10:38. But Jesus said to them, "You do not know what you are asking for. Can you drink of the cup of which I drink, or be baptized with the baptism with which I am to be baptized?"

LUKE 12:49–50. "I have come to cast fire upon the earth, and what will I but that it be kindled? But I have a baptism to be baptized with; and how distressed I am until it be accomplished!"

JOHN 17:4–5. "I have glorified thee on earth; I have accomplished the work that thou has given me to do. And now do thou, Father, glorify me with thyself, with the glory that I had with thee before the world existed."

LUKE 22:42. "Father, if thou art willing, remove this cup from me; yet not my will but thine be done."

ROMANS 5:18–19. Therefore as from the offense of the one man the result was unto condemnation to all men, so from the justice of the one the result is unto justification of life to all men. For just as by the disobedience of the one man the many were constituted sinners, so also by the obedience of the one the many will be constituted just.

EPHESIANS 5:1–2. Be you, therefore, imitators of God, as very dear children and walk in love, as Christ also loved us and delivered himself up for us an offering and a sacrifice to God to ascend in fragrant odor.

PHILIPPIANS 2:7b–8. And appearing in the form of man, he humbled himself, becoming obedient to death, even to death on a cross.

HEBREWS 5:7–9. For Jesus, in the days of his earthly life, with a loud cry and tears, offered up prayers and supplications to him who was able to save him from death, and was heard because of his reverent submission. And he, Son though he was, learned obedience from the things that he suffered; and when perfected, he became to all who obey him the cause of eternal salvation.

I have given these quotes at length to show the ethical seriousness of the Bible. The promises of the Old Testament are fufilled in the loving relationship of demand and obedience between God and man in the life and death of Christ. Men attain that salvation to the degree that they participate in Christ's submission. Hence, those who claim that religion is not ethics either have a very limited idea of the dimensions of ethics, or they have not read the Bible. The drama of salvation is cast in the ethical dimensions of life and it is to these ethical demands that the church must return if it is to be faithful.

There has always been a conspiracy against the idea that the purpose of religion is to help people be good. Other elements besides the ethical have been introduced throughout church history that have tended to deny God's ethical relationship to man. From the beginning, different non-ethical factors in religion have been successful in distracting Christians from the more difficult implementation of the command to love. First of all there was the temptation of eschatology—putting too much emphasis on the inauguration of the new kingdom with the Second Coming of Christ at the end of the world—which seemed to absolve some early Christians from their responsibilities toward this world. This attitude, still very much present in the other-world orientation of many Christians, was repeatedly condemned in both the Old and New Testaments. Whatever the blessings of the afterlife have to hold for us, the Day of the Lord will bring judgment for our actions here and now. By ignoring the needs of our neighbor, we deny the love of God for him in the here and now.

Paul's Christian converts in Salonica, shaken by the prospect of Christ's Coming, simply laid off work to wait for him. He wrote to them correcting their error. Christ's Coming was a motive for greater dedication to industrious well-doing, not a motive for avoiding it. Peter also had a few words to write on this subject. Commenting on the delay of Christ's Coming, he said:

> The Lord does not delay in his promises, but for your sake is long-suffering, not wishing that any should perish but that all should return to repentance. Seeing therefore that all these things are to be dissolved, what manner of men ought you to be in holy and pious behavior, you who await and hasten towards the coming of the day of God. But we look for new heavens and a new earth, according to his promises, wherein dwells justice. Therefore, beloved, while you look for these things, endeavor to be found by him without spot and blameless, in peace. II PETER 3:9, 11–12, 14.

Christian cult itself often provides a diversion from the ethical concerns of religion. In his First Letter to the Corinthians, Paul condemns those who find salvation in liturgy as an end in itself. His treatment of the Eucharist shows that it can be made as much an occasion of judgment as of grace:

> But in giving this charge, I do not commend you in that you meet not for the better but for the worse. For first of all I hear that when you meet in church there are divisions among you, and in part I believe it. For there must be factions, so that those

who are approved may be made manifest among you. So then when you meet together, it is no longer possible to eat the Lord's Supper. I CORINTHIANS 11:17–20.

Christian worship itself is subordinate to the demands of fraternal charity.

A more subtle, but no less real, distraction from ethics is faith. The assent of the intellect to God's love and forgiveness is a remarkably powerful and liberating experience. But one cannot stop there. The miracle of God's grace and mercy is but preparatory to his greater miracle of Christ-like action in the lives of believers. Man is not saved by his own obedience; he is saved by Christ's obedience. But he is not saved *without* his own obedience, and he must bring his own initiative and resources to bear if he is to participate in Christ's victory. James balanced the emphasis Paul put on God's initiative in our salvation by saying that man's initiative is no less necessary: "So faith, too, unless it has works, is dead in itself." (JAMES 2:17.)

Perhaps the greatest aberration from the ethical concerns of the church comes from the institutional nature of the church and its need for authority. Too often the church's resources are directed toward perpetuating its own institutions rather than serving the needs of the world. Within the Roman Church especially, conformity to human authority has been substituted for obedience to the authority of God in conscience. This has been in clear violation of Christ's teaching on the fraternal nature of authority of the church: authority is given to the community of believers to serve their needs, not to increase them. The early Christians were most conscious of the failings of human authority and attributed the murder of Christ to "the rulers of this world," i.e., the power structure of Palestine. (I CORINTHIANS 2:8.) The individual Christian, faithful to the promptings of the spirit within, sits in judgment even on the institutional church. While the church aids him in his striving for God, it is God who saves and not the church.

There are many other ways in which Christians can avoid the responsibilities of religion, attempting to place those responsibilities someplace other than the ethical dimensions of life. It is always a scandal to say that Jesus came to tell us that God is very good and therefore we must stop being bad. There is something subversive about saying that the purpose of the church is to motivate people to do good. Such a clear and simple goal does not serve to justify the multiplication of systems, ceremonies, and institutions within the church. We are asked what is unique in Christianity if it merely teaches the goodness of God and the brotherhood of men. Other religions seem to do that as well, if not better. We must answer that the purpose of Christianity is not to teach ethics, but to declare the action of God in the death, resurrection, and Coming of Christ. But since this has to do with man's relationship to God, *it must be done in the medium of ethics or it will not be done at all.* If the world does not see Christ in the actions of Christians, it will not see him at all. The dimensions in which the church is to operate are primarily in the moral—interpersonal, ethical, cultural, and historical—universe.

And so the content of religious education is not information but action, not propositions but events, not theory but conduct. The "spirituality" of religious doctrine does not arise from its being abstract or metaphysical, but from its being ethical. It is in the moral decisions of life that man exercises his Christianity and realizes his most divine potential. Religious educators have yet to accept this basic principle. They are still concerned with the forms of Christian education—the channels and techniques by which it is transmitted—and not with the content. They are still very much wrapped up in words, language, relationships, theology-as-recital, group dynamics, cult, art, and drama. These are all very fine, but they do not touch upon the critical issue in ethical formation: in ethical concerns, *what* is taught or *how* it is taught is not as important as *who teaches.*

People pattern their living upon the actions of those with whom they most strongly identify. The critical problem in religious education is not training religious people to educate, but helping the life-educators to be religious. If a young man identifies with a certain peer group, for example, the way to offer religious training is not to remove him from the group but to approach the group as such with the Christian message. The group is an excellent life-educator.

The practical consequences of the ethical orientation of religious education are evident. First of all, the church should abolish catechism classes, Sunday school, and religion classes for children. The only ones that can give religious education to children are parents. Whatever advantages arise from the formal instruction of children outside the home, they do not compensate for the abandonment of this responsibility by the parents. For too long, the churches have engaged in black-market instruction of children, taking money from people for a job that only the people can do. When it comes to religious education, children take home from class exactly what they brought from home. Why? Because in their early years they copy all their important values in life from their parents. For better or worse, parents offer nearly all of the religious education children receive. If the church wants the children, it must reach for them through the adults, and not the other way around.

The main course parents have to offer their children is the example of daily living. Children don't turn out like their parents always, but until they begin to identify with others outside the home, the behavior of parents is their main source of ethical values. A second course, the one which gives the Christian dimension to ethical formation, is the family life of worship. Since the only authentic worship for children is family worship, the parents are in the best position to train children for it. Family worship does not need to be elaborate or complicated, but it definitely needs to be stressed more. It provides the basic foundation for the liturgical life of the Christian, just as a mother's milk provides the foundation for one's digestive life. It is in family worship that there are built up the emotional, physical, and personal resources necessary for the adult life of worship. The best resources a family can use for a full life of worship are a Bible, a hymnal, and a little imagination. Worship need never be dull at home; the Bible itself provides many clues for variety in mood and expression. Also helpful may be a guide to Bible reading and a missal or prayer book. But spontaneity and frankness must always be given priority in the family's approach to God.

The formal moral training provided by the family fits in easily where there is an adequate family worship life. This formal training for children consists simply in learning and discussing the stories of the Bible. Theology-as-recital takes place best in the home. The natural discussions and comments that are made in reading the Bible stories make the most lasting impressions on young minds. To be pertinent to actual home and family situations, Bible stories need but little formal preparation on the part of the parents. The children themselves can be depended on to provide the more surprising insights.

As a person begins to look outside the home for new values and to question those he has received from his parents, the attention of the church turns from the parents as educators to the educating influences of the community: friends, neighbors, schools, playgrounds, clubs. Since all of life educates, the best religious education can be guaranteed only in the atmosphere of a dedicated community. This is why the education concerns of the church are to be directed not only toward its own institutional programs, but to the educational forces in the community. It must focus on the ethical atmosphere of the schools (all of them) first of all, and then on the recreational resources of the children. God speaks to each person through the world; this is the reason the church should expand its educational sights to include all the forces of society that contribute to the moral training of youth. These include, of course, not only youth-serving agencies, but the total life of the community. Religious education takes place in the life patterns determined by teacher salaries, classroom load, school area boundaries, segregation, academic freedom, school bonds, and other issues. Whatever is an ethical determinant is of paramount importance to religious education. Religion is taught by those who develop ethical values, whether the church likes it or not. It is the church's responsibility to support them with the insights of the Christian gospel.

The family is the most natural grouping for ethical education. As the child begins to identify with groups outside the family, the concern of religious education will swing more to those groups. It is in small groups that the most effective religious education takes place. In short, the church has to gang up in its approach to God and the world. The more natural are the groupings, the more effective they will be. By utilizing natural leadership and groupmanship, the church has an unbeatable teaching method. Call it the cell technique if you will, it works on most age groups. The formation of attitudes and habit patterns depends largely on the way we function within groups. The group approach to religious education merely utilizes the teaching function of these groups; it is the group as such, not any one individual in it, that does the teaching.

The group technique demands certain rethinking and reorganization of church programs of religious education. First of all there must be development of leadership. The ethical dimensions of religious education demand that teachers be leaders, ready to lead their groups into purposeful action. This implies a rejection of the academic approach to religious truth still dominant in Catholic religious education. Teaching is not telling, especially in ethical concerns. In religious education, the purpose of the teacher is to decrease in importance by developing the independent thought and self-reliance of the group. As students grow older, the adult leader becomes no less important, but his role becomes more and more that of a resource person representing the support given by the larger community to the activities of the group. The role of the religious educator is filled best when God's role as teacher becomes evident in the inner dynamic and interests of the group itself.

Since the purpose of religious education is to prepare people to meet God in the ethical concerns of life, its goal is more than intellectual; it must aim at the development of love. Love, to be sure, is a most complex reality. It can be defined in terms of responsibility, decisiveness, empathy, dialogue, conversation, openness, and relationship. But the Christian concept of love includes the relief of need. What *happened* between the good Samaritan and the man who fell among robbers is Jesus' description of love. Christian education is radically oriented to effective action for the relief of personal and social needs of others. It is more akin to training than teaching. Leaders cannot be content merely with imparting information or ideas, but must judge their efforts by the effectiveness of the group actions. Value in religious education is determined by what works in helping people relieve their needs.

The ethical nature of religious education demands that the size of the learning groups be kept below ten members. This demand means that many more adults will be needed as group leaders, but larger classes become unworkable as learning situations. The benefits of mass education are more apparent than real. There has been a swing in convert instruction, for example, from private instruction to class instruction, often with classes of fifty or more. In such a situation, there is more hearing taking place, but less education. In the private instruction, some dialogue between instructor and student naturally took place. But in increasing the class size indiscriminately, the dialogue has been substituted by a multiple monologue in which the instructor does not teach the group as a group but is merely addressing the individuals in it. The personal relationships between the students and the insights they have to share with one another is the most valuable teaching tool at the teacher's disposal. The class size must be small in order to utilize the group potential. It has been shown how group participation not only increases the effectiveness of the teacher, but provides the best possible situation for the development of the members as individuals. Hence, natural grouping techniques do not limit the effectiveness of the religion teacher, but expand it from a one-to-one basis to a many-to-many basis. It is in the group work approach that the human element in education is best developed. And this is precisely the object of religious education.

Natural grouping demands some changes in the local organization of religious education programs. The church and parish school are no longer the focal point of religious education but the neighborhood center—a home, meeting room, or place of business. It is important to go to people where they are in order to deal with their interests and needs. The students in public schools can split up into natural groupings (sociograms aid in doing this) and meet right in the classrooms after school hours. Most states allow school facilities to be *rented* for such purposes at a nominal fee. Older youths and adults are best organized on the basis of neighborhood, social, or vocational interests.

From the time people are able to direct themselves to ethical tasks, Christian education is *problem-centered*—directed to the relief of some answerable need. Christian teaching begins with a discussion of the problem. This usually demands preparation on the part of both leaders and members—research, inquiry, and reading. Effective action depends upon an accurate appreciation of the forces responsible for the continuation of the problem. In a problem of inadequate street lighting, for example, it is important to know not only how to acquire the lights, but what has prevented this improvement from taking place up until now. No matter what the problem is, there is usually some opposition, either organized or entrenched, which must be met to solve the problem. Often the opposition is found in the local power structure or vested interests. This opposition must be clearly recognized if action is to be effective.

Next, a plan of action must be devised. This should take up the greater part of the class time. Outside experts, resource people, the precedents of history, and the actions of other groups are needed to plan the most practical action. The final plan must be characterized by the enthusiasm and solidarity of the group. To this end it is important to reconcile differences, provide proper motivation from the word of God in the Bible, and have recourse to prayer and suitable hymns and songs. While it is the purpose of the leader-instructor to direct the group to an effective action, care must be taken to assure that it is truly the action of the group, not merely one imposed upon them.

It is not necessary that the action agreed upon be a group action, that a new action be taken at each meeting, or that it be completed before the next meeting. Individual actions are, in fact, the best, since it is through individual action that the church makes its greatest impression upon the world. It is better, for example, to decide that each member strive to organize others (outside the group) to meet a certain need rather than to have the group itself meet the need. This develops more individual initiative and involves more people in the problem. It is necessary that effective action be taken by each member and reported upon each meeting. Action is the means and the end of religious education, and failure to follow through should never be easily excused. Continuing actions are necessary for more ambitious projects. It is necessary that such actions be directed to some definite result and not be allowed to continue on and on. The satisfaction of enjoying perceptible results is necessary for the morale and success of the group. Failures there will always be, but they must be utilized as occasions of more effective planning, greater solidarity, and better execution. Christian discipline and self-denial will thereby result, not from an artificially imposed asceticism, but from the urgency and nature of the need. The reality of God's love for man must be reflected in the seriousness with which human problems are faced and solved.

The type of problems that are to be taken up, the Christian dimensions of the problems, and suggested actions are contained in the *Youth Fellowship Kit* and the *Junior Hi Kit* published yearly by the Westminster Press, Philadelphia; in the manuals published by the Young Christian Students, Young Christian Workers, and Christian Family Movement, all in Chicago; and in the *Plan of Action, Group Guidance for Grade School Apostles,* published in Notre Dame, Indiana. There are many other such publications, but these are recommended because of their definite orientation to action.

In answer to the question whether religious education must take up *social* issues, we can quote the words of Pope John in his encyclical *Mater et Magistra:*

> We reaffirm strongly that Christian social doctrine is an integral part of the Christian concept of life. On this account, we ardently desire that more and more attention be given to the study of this doctrine. In this task of communication, our beloved sons of the laity can make a great contribution. They should be convinced that the truth and efficacy of this teaching can most easily be demonstrated when they can show that it offers an effective solution for present-day difficulties. It is not enough merely to publicize a social doctrine; it has to be translated into action. Hence it is most important not only that our sons have an understanding of his social teaching, but that they be trained in it. Christian education, if it is to be called complete, should concern itself with every kind of obligation.

In reducing social principles and directives to practice, one usually goes through three stages, reviewing the actual situation, judging it in the light of these principles and directives, and deciding what can and what should be done to apply these traditional norms to the extent that the situation will permit. These three stages are usually expressed in the three terms: observe, judge, and act.

It is particularly important that young people should reflect often on this program and even more, as far as possible, follow it in practice, so that the doctrine they have learned will not be viewed merely as a set of abstract ideas but as something capable of being translated into deeds.

They should take special care, moreover, not to exhaust themselves in interminable discussions and, under pretext of seeking the better or the best, fail meanwhile to do the good that is possible and is thus obligatory (*Mater et Magistra.* New York. The American Press, 1961; 96 pp. Pp. 60–63, *passim.*).

The object of religious education is *humane action.* Whether it is directed to individual or social needs, it must be both effective and humane.

It is evident that the present situation of the church would not tolerate the type of religious formation as outlined here because of the heavy commitment of the church to the power structures of our community. Even the dedication to the building of Catholic schools has resulted in the alignment of the church hierarchy with the real estate and construction industries as well as political leaders. The effectiveness of Catholic education is being seriously questioned, not because it is not providing good education in secular subjects, but because religious education cannot take place under such heavily endowed and financially demanding circumstances. The social action that must take place in religious education is impossible in a situation where the so-called separation of church and state means non-interference of the church in social issues in return for the freedom to build church buildings and run schools. Can the church be a well-established plant and still be free to train effective Christians? Can it actually run schools on a competitive basis with public schools and be the gadfly of society?

The object of Christian education is Christian action. But what about the cultural and academic heritage of Christianity? Where is teaching to take place of criticism and appreciation of Biblical history and literature, of church history, and of the history of theology? Isn't God to be met in these studies also? Also, where is liturgical formation to take place, if not in religious education? The answer is simply that the cultural elements of Christianity are subordinate and auxiliary to ethical concerns. They are to be introduced when and where they are useful for the purpose of motivation to action. The events of the past and the promises of the future are secondary to the demand of the present. Biblical criticism and discussion, prayer and liturgy, the study of church art and music, and history are all valuable for the development of the human factor in life. But this consists mainly in the activity of decision and not aesthetical appreciation.

Group prayer and church liturgy are both complements to religious education, but not objects of it. In prayer and worship we act out in a different manner, a cultic and symbolic manner, the flow and dynamism of Christian experience. Worship is something more to be done than studied about. It is one means of expressing our relationships with God and one another. For religious education to be concerned with worship as an object of study is to digress from its real concerns. The meaning and value of worship should be immediate and apparent in the experience of it. Worship should speak clearly of God and our encounter with him. If it does not, the problem is not in lack of preparation for it in terms of academic study, but in the form of worship itself. The message imparted in liturgy must be simple and direct. If it is not, we merely end up explaining its obscurities in terms of more obscurities. Worship should be very much a part of the activity of group work—as a necessary part of Christian living. But like religious education itself, it is subordinate to the meeting with God in the decisions of life.

It is the conviction of this author that much of what is included in religious education are actually secular subjects that could easily be included in public school curricula. Biblical literature and archaeology, church history, and ecumenical concerns could be introduced as a part of our cultural heritage. Even the forms of Christian and non-Christian worship could be studied and demonstrated as a facet of comparative religion study. Such a concern would not only have a beneficial effect on public schools, but it would relieve the churches of a tremendous burden. The interfaith situation and the authority given these subjects by their treatment in school might even be more effective than the hurried and weak treatment often given them in religious education programs.

God comes to us in many ways during our life—in the appreciation of a beautiful landscape, in a scientific discovery, in the joy of music and learning, in a job well done, and in the satisfactions of health and security. But our meeting with him is always a *personal* happening, and our reaction will always be in terms of our capacity for love and self-giving, our capacity for what is most characteristically human in us. It is in our patterns of personal action and reaction that we develop the capacity to respond to God's love and demand. The God of Christians is indeed the God of truth and beauty. But more fundamentally, he is the God of ethical goodness; it is in the dimension of moral actions that we reach our deepest communication with him. The task of religious education is to prepare people to meet him by meeting the demands of his love.

CHAPTER SIX

Worship to Fit Our Needs

The Hebrews did away with religion by doing away with worship. And what the Hebrews did away with in theory, the early Christians did away with in practice. When they got together, what they did had little similarity to what others then called, or now call, worship. They didn't have churches; they met in private homes. They had no set formula to follow, no ritual that had to be complied with. Their meetings were known for their informality, the teaching that went on, and for the meal that took place. No sacrifices, no vestments, no auguries, no incense, no bowing, no complicated ceremonies. So antiliturgical were they that others felt they were an atheistic sect of some type. And this was the root of their problems with the authorities. The authorities didn't mind how God was worshiped, as long as he was. The stability of society until that time seemed to rest on an authoritarian concept of God. Religion was an asset to the ruling classes. The hostility of the early Christians to the accepted forms of worship was an attack on the structure of Roman thought and government. Christians refused to worship an authoritarian and paternalistic God, so they were thrown into jail.

The Christian rejection of worship went far back into the teaching of the Old Testament. Originally, the word "worship" was synonymous with the word "service." To worship really meant to take care of God's needs, to supply him with what he demanded—sacrifices, ceremonies, and so forth—in order to placate his hostility. In the Bible we read about the distinction made by the Hebrews between the ceremonial service offered to God and the ethical service of obedience to the law. The priority of ethical worship over ceremonial worship of God is asserted throughout the Old Testament. Ceremonial worship without the ethical service of obedience is not true worship. The prophets proclaimed that God was not pleased with the offering of sacrifices but with obedience to the law. God rewards men for what is in their hearts, not for what they do in the temple. The favors of God are promised those who perform his will; this alone is essential. Moses warned the people of Israel on the eve of their entrance into the promised land:

"If then you truly heed my commandments which I enjoin upon you today, loving and serving the LORD, your God, with all your heart and all your soul, I will give the seasonal rain to your land, the early rain and the late rain, that you may have your grain, wine and oil to gather in; and I will bring forth grass in your fields for your animals." DEUTERONOMY 11:13–14.

While the Jews spent increasingly more time, money, and personnel in the development of temple worship, there developed a school of thought that emphasized the spiritual worship of God—obedience to his demands—as contrasted and often opposed to the cultic worship. The classic expression of this view is found in the words of Samuel reprimanding King Saul for offering animal sacrifices instead of obeying the command of the Lord:

"Does the LORD delight in burnt-offerings and sacrifices
As much as in obedience to the voice of the LORD?
Behold, to obey is better than sacrifice,
And to hearken, than the fat of rams.
For the sin of divination is rebellion,
And the iniquity is of the teraphim is arrogance.
Because you have rejected the word of the LORD,
He has rejected you from being king." I SAMUEL 15:22–23.

As the theology of the Hebrews developed, it seemed to extol more and more the importance of man's ethical relationship to God:

> Sacrifice or oblation you wished not,
> but ears open to obedience you gave me.
> Holocausts or sin-offerings you sought not;
> then said I, "Behold I come;
> in the written scroll it is prescribed for me,
> To do your will, O my God, is my delight,
> and your law is in my heart!" PSALMS 40:7–9.

It was left to the writers of the wisdom literature, who seemed relieved of all cultic concerns, to identify obedience as participation in the wisdom of God and the greatest gift to be received from his hands. Such is the thought of this poetic praise of wisdom-obedience found in the Book of Job:

> But when can wisdom be obtained,
> and where is the place of understanding?
> Man knows nothing to equal it,
> nor is it to be had in the land of the living.
> Solid gold cannot purchase it,
> nor can its price be paid with silver. . . .
> God knows the way to it;
> it is he who is familiar with its place. . . .
> When he made rules for the rain
> and a path for the thunderbolts,
> Then he saw wisdom and appraised it,
> gave it its setting, knew it through and through.
> And to man he said:
> Behold, the fear of the LORD is wisdom;
> and avoiding evil is understanding.
> JOB 28:12–15, 23, 26–28.

The Jews never disowned their cultic tradition, however; they came to accept it as one form of response to God's command. For this reason, the Jews were able to continue their tradition and indulge in their love for ritual until the destruction of the temple in 70 A.D. But what the Jews did not disown formally, Christ did. He placed himself solidly in the prophetical school which gives the inward conformity to God's will absolute primacy. He did not renounce cult so much as completely ignore it; he felt that the controversy between cult and ethic had been long solved in Hebrew literature. Like many of his ascetical contemporaries, he had little to do with the worship in the temple. But more than any of the former prophets or contemporary teachers, he identified the service of God with the service of the neighbor. The ultimate concern of religion is not cult but the love-ethic:

> And behold, a certain lawyer got up to test him, saying, "Master, what must I do to gain eternal life?" But he said to him, "What is written in the Law? How dost thou read?" He answered and said, "Thou shalt love the Lord thy God with thy whole heart, and with thy whole soul, and with thy whole strength, and with thy whole mind: and thy neighbor as thyself." And he said to him, "Thou hast answered rightly; do this and thou shalt live." But he, wishing to justify himself, said to Jesus, "And who is my neighbor?"
>
> Jesus answered, "A certain man was going down from Jerusalem to Jericho and he fell in with robbers, . . ." LUKE 10:25–30.

Every act of kindness and service directed to the need of the neighbor is an act of worship of God, even when performed by nonbelievers, winning eternal salvation:

> "Then the just will answer him, saying, 'Lord, when did we see thee hungry, and feed thee; or thirsty, and give thee drink? And when did we see thee a stranger, and take thee in; or naked, and clothe thee? Or when did we see thee sick, or in prison, and come to thee?' And answering the king will say to them, 'Amen I say to you, as long as you did it for one of these, the least of my brethren, you did it to me.'" MATTHEW 25:37–40.

Human need alone identifies a person as the neighbor; human need alone is sufficient claim on the charity of those who can relieve it. No other credentials are required because God is in those needs and is served in them.

Christ verified the relative need for cultic expression of religious beliefs. Worship is not condemned as useless, but its value is determined entirely by the degree of support it offers the life of human service. Christ made worship completely functional, a means to the end of ethical progress. He did not deny that God comes to man in worship. But he did stress that God comes to man in all the situations of life, no less than in worship. Worship itself is a secular need, arising from man's creaturely need for expressing himself in prayer, song, and ceremony—a need which Christ would not deny to man. But, as all other life activities, it must serve man's struggle for humanity and not oppose it. Christ did away with the absolute and indispensable nature of worship. A ceremony or prayer is of value only insofar as it promotes the advance of God's kingdom by encouraging people to be more concerned. Christ's choice of the cultic signs, or sacraments, of the new covenant express his identification of God's will with service rendered the neighbor. The elemental human actions of washing, eating, consoling, healing, encouraging, reconciling, and marrying are directed toward the need of the neighbor. It is only by the later accretions from Roman and other cultures that the horizontal and fraternal nature of the sacraments takes on the vertical and authoritarian expression of a remote God. In giving his church the sacraments, Christ directed worship toward the bodily needs of the neighbor in the most concrete manner possible. Fraternal service is the Christian worship, worship in spirit and in truth; the distinction between the religious and the secular, the world of God and the world of man, the service of God and the service of man, is demolished. The love-ethic alone is the criterion by which Christ's followers are to be judged, not their relationship to ceremonies of religion. Worship is useful only as it helps people be responsible to the needs of men.

The apostles saw Christ's rejection of the absolute need for worship as a natural fulfillment of an accepted school of Hebrew thought. Christ came to fulfill the Law, not found another religion. For men of the Bible, religion meant a system of worship. Now that cultic worship is overshadowed by the demands of love, the apostle James could write: "Religion pure and undefiled before God the Father is this: to give aid to orphans and widows in the tribulation, and to keep oneself unspotted from this world." (JAMES 1:27.) This teaching is not so surprising to those familiar with the tradition of prophets such as Micah:

> You have been told, O man, what is good,
> and what the LORD requires of you:
> Only to do the right and to love goodness,
> and to walk humbly with your God. MICAH 6:8.

The ethical nature of the new movement was expressed in the freedom of the Christian assemblies. The good news of salvation was not to be dampened by imposing regulations upon the activities of the Christian assemblies. The only rule to be followed was that of mutual consideration for one another's needs. The good news made a priest out of every individual; every man is his own liturgist and theologian. He has a right to express his faith in the presence and power of God in his life in whatever way he determines is appropriate. Paul was most explicit in supporting the demands of the individual's conscience in matters of Christian practice and ceremony:

> Let not him who eats despise him who does not eat, and let not him who does not eat judge him who eats; for God has received him. Who art thou to judge another's servant? To his own lord he stands or falls; but he will stand, for God is able to make him stand. For one esteems one day above another; another esteems every day alike. Let everyone be convinced in his

own mind. He who regards the day, regards it for the Lord; and he who eats, eats for the Lord, for he gives thanks to God. . . . For the kingdom of God does not consist in food and drink, but in justice and peace and joy in the Holy Spirit; for he who in this way serves Christ pleases God and is approved by men. ROMANS 14:3–6, 17–18.

The regulations set down by the apostles were based on respect for the needs of the individual. Any restrictions on the free expressions of the Holy Spirit were directed only to make that freedom more available and obvious to all. A famous case, both now and at the time of the apostles, is that of the glossolalia, a kind of inspired gibberish which expresses the freedom enjoyed by the Christian. While Paul claimed in his First Epistle to the Corinthians that this form of worship is less perfect than the more intellectual expressions of faith and that it somewhat upset the meetings, he defended them as appropriate expressions of the presence of the Holy Spirit who dwelt in the most ignorant believers. Even though he proposed that all strive for the more perfect gifts to edify the whole congregation and visitors, instead of only oneself, he refuses to outlaw this individualistic form of witness. The early church's tolerance of the glossolalia testifies to the prior consideration that must be given to the needs of the individual in worship. Worship is for man, and man is first of all an individual. Praying with the understanding—to the edification of the congregation—is desirable. Praying with the spirit—for the edification of oneself—is indispensable. The only restriction Paul laid upon the practice was that not everybody speak in tongues at once but "by twos or at most threes," in turn. "For God is a God of peace not of disorder." (I CORINTHIANS 14:27, 33.)

The early Christians felt free to worship God wherever and however they felt. Each man was free to act according to his own conscience as long as he preserved due regard for the conscience and sensitivities of others. Even in the

Eucharist, there was little regulation. Elements from services of the Jewish synagogue and sacred meals were freely employed, old psalms and new hymns were sung, the teaching of the apostles was read and studied, and there was no doubt much discussion and debate. The fervor and spontaneity of the early Christian gatherings were an abundant source of freedom and strength, as we read in the Acts of the Apostles:

> And they continued steadfastly in the teaching of the apostles and in the communion of the breaking of the bread and in the prayers. And continuing daily with one accord in the temple, and breaking bread in their houses, they took their food with gladness and simplicity of heart, praising God and being in favor with all the people. And day by day the LORD added to their company such as were to be saved. ACTS 2:42, 46–47.

For a couple hundred years there was no set formula for Mass. And it was even much later when the Mass was standardized for the Roman Church. The early believers improvised their celebrations, using the basic meal of bread and wine. The one consistent element we find in Christian worship is its variety of forms. The bond of unity between Christians was freedom of spirit. External observances were expressions of interior freedom, not of outward regulation.

The stereotyped patterns of worship today and the rigid control of ceremonies by the hierarchy seems to completely deny the freedom once experienced by Christians. Most Catholics still feel that some official regulation is needed to validate every authentic cultic act. Liturgy is regarded as ceremonies drawn up by professional liturgists to be performed by local congregations. The church has come full circle to the idolization of cult once so strongly rejected by the prophets and Christ. If a person wanted to fashion a form of worship depicting and honoring a remote and authoritarian God, he could do no better than copy the present Roman liturgy. Nowhere in the church is paternalism more in control than in the matter of worship. Even the aims of the liturgical movement fail to express the greatest need in worship: freedom. The present innovations are being imposed upon the people in the same high-handed fashion as in the past. The first aim of the reform of worship is not new rites or regulations but the development of Christian initiative and responsibility in worship. This development can only take place in freedom.

The key to the reform of the church is the understanding that worship is not the ultimate concern of the church. The proclamation of the God of Christ is expressed first of all through Christian action, secondly through education, and lastly through worship. Liturgy is not the norm of Christian faith but its expression; people are not to believe what they are doing in church, but what they do in church should express what they believe. Neither should worship be used as a substitute for religious education. There is the feeling among many liturgists that once we have a truly popular liturgy, then will arise a truly Christian people. The great investment in our churches and ceremonies of worship will be justified only if we can make the ceremonies more meaningful to the people. But the experience of the Protestants has taught them that dramatic worship is no substitute for the painstaking work and individual attention demanded by religious education. What the people bring to worship—by way of secular commitment and religious formation—is perhaps more important than what they receive from it. The liturgy of the church will become relevant as soon as the faith becomes relevant.

It is surprising how much and how poorly Catholics pray. Because of the emphasis on institutional conformity and approved prayers, Catholics don't take themselves seriously in their prayers. Faith teaches that God comes to us in response to our needs; prayer must begin with the expression of *our* needs. Catholics pray lots, but rarely speak of their own needs in their prayer. If asked to pray, most of them would say an Our Father or a Hail Mary, which certainly identifies their Catholicity, but says little about their proficiency at prayer. Children in parochial schools spend much time in endless repetition of the standard formulized prayers. Because these prayers usually have so little meaning for the students, their attention is usually suspended in a reverential distraction. Such non-prayer only alienates them from the benefits of prayer. This situation might not be so bad if only children were limited to a few formulized prayers. But the same is true of adults, priests, and nuns. If the strength of their faith is determined by their ability to speak freely to God about their needs and his mercies, then it is time to question the effectiveness of their religious formation.

Prayer must ask for things. Catholics pray poorly because they ask too little and halfheartedly. They have not completely grown out of the idea that prayer must be directed to strictly religious concerns—such as the conversion of a friend—or a special intervention of God in the physical order of things. Most people cannot take religious needs too seriously for any length of time. They have learned by experience that God is not performing miracles any more, at least for them. They have never been taught about God's intervention in all the *ordinary* events of life, especially the interpersonal ones. They have not yet learned that their actual concerns are also God's concerns and are the best raw material for meaningful, and even exciting, prayer.

The desire for popularity, the attention of a loved one, financial security, scholastic or athletic success, health, cars, good surf, racial harmony, the success of a dinner dance, and church reform are proper foundations for a personal relationship with God. A Christian is a person who wants something. He brings strong feelings to his prayer and honestly expresses them. He does not ask for the universal good of mankind, but for the particular and concrete goods needed by real people. Felt needs are the doorway of our contact with God. Whatever does not proceed from a sense of urgency and need is not religious, but probably the expression of self-satisfaction. The stronger we feel about the concerns we bring to our prayer, the more credit we give to God. He who asks much loves much, because he trusts much. Worship must be first of all honest; the first requirement is to know thyself, to admit not only one's inadequacy and faults, but more important, one's aspirations and concerns.

Often our prayer is faulty because our lives are faulty. If we are indifferent to the needs of others or find it impossible to involve ourselves in the vital issues around us, our prayer will be as dull as our life. Involvement brings significance to prayer. One can pray best when he is up to his neck in controversy or an important project. The tasks and needs for which people assemble to take responsibility are the proper objects of their prayer. What brings them together is what brings them before God. Whether it be some recreational need, a poverty problem, or a political need, it is the opening for a new relationship with God.

Prayer often begins with the desire for physical needs. It should develop into a desire for man's greatest need: personal responsibility. It is in this gift that man finds the answers to his needs. Our basic human needs call for basic human answers: initiative, creativity, perseverence, organization. God's great gifts are in this realm of action and relationships. His greatest miracles are not performed by interfering with the laws of physical nature but by bringing men to make the right decisions. Our petitions for God's aid should include a plea for the strength to do what the situation demands. The great works of God are witnessed in the accomplishments of education, technology, community development, and political reform. It is to such deeds our prayers must direct us.

The worship of the Christian is both individual and social because it is humane. The individual and social needs of men are the occasions of private and common prayer. Our worship life is all of a piece; facility on one level of worship prepares us for facility on another. But because all prayer must be personal—that is, sprung from felt needs—proficiency at private prayer is a prerequisite for prayer at other levels. The authenticity of public prayer demands that people know how to pray as individuals. They cannot be united in a unity of spirit and purpose if they do not take their individual needs seriously. The power of group prayer depends on the total urgency felt by the individuals. For this reason, liturgical reform must begin with the fulfillment of Christ's demand: "But when thou prayest, go into thy room, and closing thy door, pray to thy Father in secret; and thy Father, who sees in secret, will reward thee." (MATTHEW 6:6.)

Since prayer is an experiential event, success demands experimentation. Sometimes it serves to have a prayer group whose purpose is to learn how to pray together. Such a project is described in books like *Two or Three Together* by Harold W. Freer and Francis B. Hall (New York: Harper and Row, Publishers, 1954. 187 pp.). But like group dynamics experiments, prayer groups are preparation for prayer in other interest groups. Prayer cannot be a legitimate concern in itself for any length of time. Prayer groups break up and the members are able to lead other interest groups in meaningful worship.

It is a time for experimentation on all levels of worship, especially in the official worship of the parish. This is no time for writing new liturgies. Catholics especially are in no position to compose official liturgies; for too long they have been following rubrics instead of worshiping. It is time to look around at what other religions are doing, assessing the great variety of forms of worship, both Christian and non-Christian, and preparing the way for the acceptance of a great variety of liturgical forms in the Roman Church. An indispensable demand of ecumenical unity will be not only to recognize the authenticity of other forms of cult, but to allow their use and implementation within the Roman Church. In no area of the church is control and centralization less needed or demanded by tradition than worship. The unity of the church is recognized in the variety of forms demanded by the freedom of the human spirit, not in external regulations.

A great need is participation of the membership in the planning of worship. The fraternity of God is best expressed by the ability of all to contribute to the common expression of prayer. In a parish this becomes practical in the forming of a committee that aids the pastor in the planning of the services. The needs of the congregation can be remembered in the prayers for the people by filling out cards on entering church. The whole service should reflect the general needs of the local church, the local community, and the larger needs of society. A pastor needs help to keep up with the live and significant issues.

Language, ceremonies, and vestments must be modern. Rigid insistence on the symbolism of past ages only tells us that the church is old, a rather secondary value today. Contemporary expressions of the church's message are demanded by the ethical orientation of religion. Whatever is foreign, out-of-date, or abstruse only alienates men from God. The music, gestures, architecture, decorations, and language must speak to men where they are. New forms of communication are needed in church: movies, TV, sound tapes, dance, choral speaking, drama, debates, and musical productions. The whole field of communications will become more important to the church as it awakens to its task of persuasion. Once communication, and not control, is seen as the means to build the kingdom of God, then the talents of poets, artists, musicians, folk dancers and folk singers, and writers will find more room for expression in the church. The most creative minds of the world are only repelled by the present rigidity of the church. The church must again make room for God's prophets. As it is now, not even the creative potential within the church is able to find expression there, so lacking is the church in internal freedom. In allowing the people to develop whatever form of worship they choose, the clergy would lose nothing except their own ineffectiveness in building up a worshiping community.

The greatest obstacle to liturgical reform is the lack of liberty within the church. Another obstacle is the breakdown of religious education and knowledge of the Bible. Christians traditionally identified with the experiences of the people of the Bible. But the Bible is still an unknown factor in Catholic life, its theology remote and suspect. The Bible should be their chief liturgical text. Instead of being offered as a basic book of prayer and inspiration for private and common use, it is still parceled out most judiciously—heavy on the texts supporting the primacy of Peter and the apostles. Reforms are already being worked out by professional liturgists amplifying the use of the Bible in worship. But until the church generously gives the *whole* Bible to be used as place and circumstances dictate, Catholic worship will remain less than Christian. No liturgical committee in Washington is competent to arrange worship services for the unlimited situations across the land. Suggestions for Bible readings according to the liturgical year, holidays, and other occasions should be provided, but the responsibility of the actual choice of texts must belong to the local congregation. For any single feast, a wide variety of texts are appropriate. Freedom of choice develops both familiarity and responsibility.

A free use of the Bible in Sunday worship is no substitute for religious education or strong family worship. Catholic unfamiliarity with Biblical theology can hardly be remedied by throwing more texts at them. Religious formation is primarily the task of religious education. Neither does a brief contact with the Bible at Sunday Mass develop a dependence upon the Bible in one's prayer life. The effectiveness of the use of the Bible in common worship depends directly on the appreciation and insight brought to worship by each individual. The promotion of the Bible in home and private prayer is indispensable for a strongly theological parish worship. The great mass of Catholics cannot attend daily Mass or vespers to receive their liturgical formation. The official worship of the church must be brought into their homes; there is great need for a new Book of Common Prayer that will make the worship life of the church accessible to every Christian wherever he is. A real dedication to the development of the prayer life of Christians demands that the official worship of the church not be assigned exclusively to clerics and religious personnel. Neither is there any justification for limiting access to liturgical life to those able to attend daily Mass.

The central place of the Bible in worship is expressed not only in the use of readings from the Bible but also in the influence of Biblical theology in the hymns, prayers, and sermons. The old Calvinists went so far as to refuse to sing any hymn that was not taken right out of the Bible. Archbishop Cranmer was careful in remodeling the collects of the Roman missal according to the best scriptural theology of his day. The order of worship for the Eucharist as found in the new Methodist, Lutheran, Presbyterian, and proposed Episcopalian services displays much fidelity to tradition as well as to the theology of the Bible. With Biblical theology available as a source of unity, an order of worship that is truly common to all Christian communions has suddenly become a practical possibility.

One of the important contributions of Cranmer's Book of Common Prayer was the replacement of a faith-in-miracles by a faith-in-God theology. The function of those Christians who have died before us is not just to act as our intercessors before a reluctant and suspicious God, but to stand as witnesses to the presence of God in their lives and the lives of others doing his bidding. The saints are much more present to us as models and exemplars than as front-office secretaries dispensing religious commodities. The contrast between the two approaches can be seen in the comparison of the collects for the Feast of All Saints. The Roman liturgy has:

Almighty and Everlasting God, since you have given us one feast day to celebrate the merits of all your saints, we ask you through their combined intercession to give us the fullness of the mercy we long for.

The Book of Common Prayer has:

O Almighty God, who hast knit together thine elect in one communion and fellowship, in the mystical body of thy Son Christ our Lord: Grant us grace so to follow thy blessed Saints in all virtues and godly living, that we may come to those unspeakable joys, which thou hast prepared for them that unfeignedly love thee.

The sacraments are the uniquely Christian form of worship. They are the official cultic signs of the church. They are expressions of the life of Christians. They are not related to death, the afterworld, or the metaphysical subworld. They point to life, specifically human life as it was intended by Christ to be lived. The supernatural character of the sacraments does not come from their ability to cause miracles in the physical or metaphysical order, but from the faith that they express, a faith in the ethical God revealed and known in Christ. The sacraments are ceremonies intended to express and support our commitment to God's presence in human living.

The sacraments are not properly prayers, though we have become accustomed to think of them as rather lengthy prayers. They are actions, or more properly events. Christian life is a life of works, not a state of being or matter of words. Its formal worship is made of things to be done, a manner of experience modern man is just beginning to relearn. Authenticity in the sacraments demands a putting away of the forms and rubrics of the past in order to seek and find valid expressions of the faith of modern man. Contemporary man must find new creedal forms of dogma to express his own grasp of the faith; he must also find new forms of cultic expression. The Nicene Creed accurately expresses the faith of a third-century Christian, but not that of a twentieth-century Christian. The rites of past ages express little of what modern Christians experience in their contact with Christ. Tradition demands not an adherence to the external forms of past ages, but a honest attention to and expression of God's word today. The church needs new cult-actions.

Baptism is the sacrament of initiation into the Christian faith. Because of the intellectual nature of faith, baptism has been associated with the work of religious formation. The baptism of adults comes as the climax of a rather thorough and intense preparation. The baptism of infants, on the other hand, is the pledge of the family and the rest of the Christian community to provide the Christian nurture and environment required for the development of the Christian adult. At present, the rite of baptism is accompanied by exorcisms, anointings, and prayers that have little relationship to faith or the Christian community. The tendency of the past years has been to emphasize the bestowal of metaphysical grace and its mystical qualities. This represents a quest for greater understanding of the rites, but misses the more basic meaning which must be presented in much more straightforward terms.

Baptism represents an acceptance of the God revealed in Christ. As such, it is directly related to ethical, not philosophical or ontological, values. It is a baptism for the remission of sins, declaring the presence of God in man's ethical progress. It represents a conversion from wrong to right, from evil to good, from indifference to concern, from paternalism to brotherhood, from isolation to involvement in the needs of the neighbor. The consciousness of God's commitment to man can only take the form of membership in the community dedicated to the development of man.

The present rite and situation of baptism express a removal from the human situation rather than a dedication to it. It is almost a secret ceremony performed in the presence of a few relatives and friends in an empty church. The Christian community hardly knows what is taking place, much less appreciates its own role implied in the ceremony. The rites and circumstances of baptism should rather speak of the community's acceptance of the newly baptized. A suitable occasion for baptism would be a time when a sizable number of parishioners are present—after religion classes on Saturday or during the week, before evening Mass, or connected with meetings of parish membership. It is a rite of initiation into the community dedicated to God's purposes. The prayers must be clear and to the point, speaking of the terms of Christian commitment.

Confirmation is supposed to be the sacrament of apostolic dedication. At present it merely marks the end of the primary courses in religion. It most often represents the termination of all formal instruction in the faith. The practice in America of confirming at age twelve supports the conviction of the students that their catechism course is over. They generally feel, with justification, that the further courses offered to junior high and high school students are merely amplifications of the answers of the catechism. The futility of giving secondary students the same academic treatment they received in grammar school is evident in their rejection of religious education. It is to be questioned whether this is due to the competition from school and teen activities or to the failure to cope with their personal and ethical needs.

Whatever cultic forms are used to embellish the rites of baptism and confirmation, they should speak clearly of the educational responsibilities of the church. These sacraments of initiation should be events of renewed dedication to the task of Christian nurture. The grace they confer is an interpersonal reality that must be mediated through the intelligent commitment and labor of the whole community and especially of the family. By means of group action parents should be prepared for the responsibilities of Christian parenthood. Their presence and participation in the sacraments of baptism and confirmation demand full attention to their need for in-service training as the children grow up. The parish as a whole must be organized to support the family in its unique task of religious formation and development. Rather than taking parents away from the activities necessary for religious leadership and example, parish programs should direct the parents to them.

Baptism and confirmation do not remove the Christian from the world, but set him down right in the middle of it as God's witness. If the fire of Pentecost is ever to take over the lives of our young, we must become much more dedicated to the development of a living faith that is expressed in actions instead of answers. Baptism and confirmation mean that the church promises to train its young to go out and do God's word.

Penance is the sacrament of our reconciliation with God, not God's reconciliation with us. God has not left us in our sin although we have tried to leave him. God has no grievance against us; it is we who have the grievance against him. Sin consists not in offending God, but in acting as if he could be offended, in denying his ethical nature. Sin lies in the deformity caused in the sinner, not in the offense offered God. The sinner has missed the mark because of the harm he has done to himself first of all, and only secondarily to other persons. Christ entered this world to tell us that no man is to judge another in this life for God himself does not judge in this life. "For God did not send his Son into the world in order to judge the world, but that the world might be saved through him." (JOHN

3:17.) Christ came to heal man's deformity, not to bring God's judgment on the world. God's judgment, in fact, is present in the sin itself, which is its own punishment: "He who believes in him is not judged; but he who does not believe is already judged, because he does not believe in the name of the only-begotten Son of God. Now this is the judgment: The light has come into the world, yet men have loved the darkness rather than the light, for their works were evil." (JOHN 3:18–19.) The basis of all sin is the rejection of God's goodness as revealed in Christ. The resurrection is the manifestation of that goodness and those who reject it have already suffered the punishment: "And when he [the Advocate] has come he will convict the world of sin, and of justice, and of judgment: of sin, because they do not believe in me; of justice, because I go to the Father, and you will see me no more; and of judgment, because the prince of this world has already been judged." (JOHN 16:8–11.) The only judgment men will experience is the goodness of God, which will expose the darkness of men's acts.

The teaching of Christ is in complete contrast to the primitive idea of God's being put out with man. Christ left us with no doubt about it: God refuses to be our enemy, in this life or the next. He came to restore man's moral wholeness by his insistence on the moral perfection of God. Sin is an illness to be healed as a physical illness is healed. Christ was harsh only with those who denied the love of God: "Why are you arguing these things in your hearts? Which is it easier, to say to the paralytic, 'Thy sins are forgiven thee,' or to say, 'Arise, and take up thy pallet, and walk'?" (MARK 2:8–9.) While forgiveness is a special action of God in each individual case, this action produces no change in God from a state of an aggrieved person to a non-aggrieved person, but it does produce a change in the person forgiven from a person who feels God has a grievance against him to a person who knows that such is not so.

Repentance for the wrong done is the condition for the grace of knowing God's oneness and presence with the sinner. God's forgiveness changes man's relationship with God from one of suspicion to one of openness and acceptance of God's benevolent concerns.

The basis of the ancient religions was the anger of God. Cult and sacrifice were the means employed to propitiate his wrath. The New Testament writers rejected the whole idea of sacrifice, not because the sacrifices of antiquity were insufficient or imperfect, but because the very idea of sacrifice predicated a hostility in God. The sacrifice of Christ was actually no sacrifice, but the reverent submission of Christ to the will of his Father, especially in the acceptance of his death. The Epistle to the Hebrews makes this clear; the new covenant is inaugurated not by a successful sacrifice but by the revelation of God's goodness in the ethical perfection of Christ's death:

> For Jesus, in the days of his earthly life, with a loud cry and tears, offered up prayers and supplications to him who was able to save him from death, and was heard because of his reverent submission. And he, Son though he was, learned obedience from the things he suffered; and when perfected, he became to all who obey him the cause of eternal salvation called by God a high priest according to the order of Melchisedech.
>
> Therefore in coming into the world, he says, "Sacrifice and oblation thou wouldst not, but a body thou has fitted to me: In holocausts and sin-offerings thou hast had no pleasure. Then said I, 'Behold, I come—(in the head of the book it is written of me) —to do thy will, O God.'" In saying in the first place, "Sacrifices and oblations and holocausts and sin-offerings thou wouldst not, neither hast thou had pleasure in them" (which are offered according to the Law), and then saying, "Behold, I come to do thy will, O God," he annuls the first covenant in order to establish the second. It is in this "will" that we have been sanctified through the offering of the body of Jesus Christ once for all.
>
> Thus also the Holy Spirit testifies unto us. For after having said, "This is the covenant that I will make with them after those

days, says the Lord: I will put my laws upon their hearts, and upon their minds I will write them," he then adds, "And their sins and their iniquities I will remember no more." Now where there is forgiveness of these, there is no longer offering for sin. HEBREWS 5:7–10; 10:5–10, 15–18.

In this rabbinical dissertation, the author is only saying that God forgives freely, without demanding any special services or sacrifices. There is to be no penalty attached to conversion from wrong to right. The only condition demanded by God for forgiveness is the penitence of the sinner, his admission of guilt and the turning to a new way of life. In the conversion we share in the ethical accomplishment of Christ's obedience in dying for us. In the resurrection and triumph of Christ we have the pledge of God's forgiveness, which will be freely given to those who turn from their sin to the new way offered by God.

In giving the apostles the power to forgive sins, Christ was not replacing the sacrifices and sin offerings of antiquity with a new rite of confession. This would have involved no new relationship between God and man, no advance in man's appreciation of God. Christ was releasing man from an obligation, not placing a new one upon him. The task of the church is to declare, pronounce, and assert God's immediate forgiveness to all those who are repentant. The Christian practice of confession of sins was a response to a felt need; it was not an obligation that created a new need. Neither Christ nor the apostles intended that confession and penance be imposed as an obligation upon sinners as a condition for forgiveness. The church, in its official ministry, is to mediate God's forgiveness to man; but this does not entail the interposition of a new rite. Men are the mediators for all of God's relationships with men. We come to know God's forgiveness only through the words and deeds of other men. But the Christian dispensation does not demand that this mediation take the form of a rite. Rather the rite of confession is subordinate to the mediating function of the church, pointing to the task of the church to declare God's forgiveness of all men, not just those who receive the sacrament. The sacrament serves to declare God's freedom and gratuitous mercy, not his arbitrary imposition of a new demand.

The early Christians knew that forgiveness was free. The only requirements were ethical ones, not cultic ones. A man merely had to regret the wrong that he had done to be the object of a special and personal act of God drawing him into a most personal relationship. In speaking of the purity of heart demanded for the reception of Holy Communion, Paul wrote, "But let a man prove himself, and so let him eat of that bread and drink of the cup; for he who eats and drinks unworthily, without distinguishing the body, eats and drinks judgment to himself." (I CORINTHIANS 11:28–29.) Confession of sins was entirely voluntary. Scholars have traced for us the many different forms of confession that have existed in the history of the church and the various disciplines and doctrines used to support them. The only thing about which we can be sure is that the forms of penitential discipline are relative to the needs of the time. The most consistent element in the practice of the church has been the change and adaptation of the forms of the sacraments. To hold that the present penitential discipline and theology is an absolute standard that cannot be varied is to step out of the living tradition of the church, which attempts to fit the grace of the gospel to the needs of men.

The present practice of the church is characterized by 1) the church laws that oblige a person to confess his mortal sins to a priest before receiving Communion and 2) the attributing of the efficacy of the sacrament to the absolution prayer recited by the priest. Neither of these elements is demanded by revelation or the tradition of the church. In my opinion, the external obligations attached to confession tend to deny the freedom of God in forgiving and the freedom he gives in forgiving. In the area dealing with the fact of God's mercy, the church cannot afford to impose new obligations. Auricular confession should be something available for those who feel a need for it. The general confession and absolution at Mass and other ceremonies should suffice for the sacramental needs of most people. The main burden of our penitential life should lie in our private and family prayers where the forgiveness of God is also available. Private confession to a priest should be voluntary, as it was during a considerable portion of church history. In times of crisis, special sorrow, or special grace, the priest is available for special confession. It would be hoped that the counsel and direction he gives would aptly express the relevance of the gospel to the needs of the penitent.

New forms of penance will have to be developed if the church is to proclaim man's need for forgiveness and God's mercy in freely giving it. Penance is much more than a spiritual service station for grace. It is more than an occasion of putting oneself back into a state in which forgiveness is no longer required; it certainly should not be an occasion for validating one's righteousness and being out of debt with God. It must simply be the expression of our turning away from sin to the new life opened to us by God's forgiveness and demand.

Christ gave us a meal of bread and wine to serve as a cultic aid to keep alive what he did and taught. The simplicity of this rite was meant to be the sign of the immediacy of God's presence with us. No big churches, vestments, candles, altar stones, choirs, or commentators necessary, just bread and wine on a table. God is not found in great ceremonies but in the gladness of breaking bread together. This earthy meal was intended by Christ to be the ultimate expression of the ethical nature of his religion. The sharing of the bread and wine brings to mind the death of Christ; it portrays God's presence in man's life; and it points out the needs man must serve.

The meal intended to express the simplicity of Christian living, Christians have managed to overload with the most arcane and extravagant accessories. What once expressed God's accessibility now expresses his unapproachability. The saying of Mass in a simple chapel is governed by volumes of regulations and requirements that militate against the spontaneity and simplicity intended by Christ. There has developed a whole industry of church goods suppliers who make millions yearly providing the sacred appurtenances for worship. The Eucharist was intended to turn man to his brother; now it turns him to the Eucharistic establishment and its demands. Christians assemble at Mass not to serve the living God but the dictates of the ritual and the latest liturgical maxim.

The Eucharist has assumed a great variety of forms during the history of the church. The task of liturgical reform is to give the Eucharist new forms that speak more directly to the needs of modern man. So far, the reforms attempting to bring the Mass closer to the people have merely tried to accommodate the scholarship regarding the Mass to the present Eucharistic discipline. The rigid control of the Eucharistic rites has passed from the control of the pope to national councils of bishops, but the control remains. Modern languages have been introduced into the rites, but the rites remain a long series of prayers instead of a meal to be shared. The people have been allowed to participate in the ceremonies, only to find out that the ceremonies are meaningless to the twentieth century. In the concrete working out of a new liturgy, the academic studies of liturgists have offered little aid in developing Christian worship.

Catholics have substituted rubrics for worship for so long that they have forgotten that worship is an experiential event, one that must develop from the doing of it. There are no patterns of worship provided in the liturgies of the past or the proposals of the present that can answer man's worship needs today. We are in no position to be writing new liturgies, we know so little about worship. It would be best for us to drop all the legislation governing worship and begin where we are. With a priest, a few people around a table, a loaf of bread, a cup of wine, a Bible and a few good hymns, we might be able to discover what Christ asked us to do in memory of him. From there we might be able to build up some form of worship for larger groups, if that indeed becomes necessary. But today the utility of parish worship itself is called into question. Perhaps there is no longer need for parish churches and Sunday Mass.

The sacrament of the Anointing of the Sick used to be called Extreme Unction and was administered only to the dying. It has undergone much reform in the last few years; besides being put into the vernacular, it can be administered to the ill even if there is no immediate indication of dying. It is presented now not as the sacrament of the dying but of the sick. This change may not seem too far-reaching, but it does indicate a return to a more Christian attitude toward illness and our human situation in general. Now the purpose of the sacrament is not so much to prepare an ill person for his entry into heaven, but to aid his faith and help him find God's goodness even in the midst of pain.

Illness brings a religious, as well as a physical and psychological, crisis. People tend to feel that God is getting back at them for something; their unfaith comes out. They feel that something is wrong between them and God. The purpose of the church's ministrations and the comfort and care given to the sick is to mediate God's love for them. Sickness does not mean that something is wrong with the world or with God. But the inability to face this crisis may indicate that something is wrong with men in their relationship to one another. The church attempts to help people solve for themselves the great riddle of pain and death by bringing them in contact with the mercy and care of God.

The ministry of Christ and the apostles to the sick was a sign that the kingdom of God was come. Christ took people's bodies and their bodily needs seriously; God loves people as body-people. Unless God loves us in our present situation, he doesn't love us at all. The one thing a sick person wants is to get well. It's hard to communicate with him unless one is attending to that predominant need. The only way Christians can mediate God's love to the ill is to try to heal them.

During a long period of time, the church forgot this lesson. It actually opposed the progress of medical science. In 529, Emperor Justinian was persuaded by church officials to close the medical schools of Athens and Alexandria. In 1215, the church condemned surgery and forbade priests to practice it. In 1248 the dissection of the human body was pronounced sacrilegious and the study of anatomy was banned. This great breach between medicine and religion, and the general suspicion of the body, continued down almost to our own time. A few religious communities since the Middle Ages have taken upon themselves the service of the sick. But even today there is the impression that the church runs hospitals primarily as a proselytizing venture. The lack of commitment of the church as a whole to the relief of the sick is seen in the way it is left to the sisters in the hospitals. The sacrament of the Anointing of the Sick should proclaim the dedication of the whole church to healing and the progress of medicine.

The object of the sacrament of the sick is not the fear of death or the afterlife. The church spends so much time speaking about the afterworld that it does not equip people to deal with the problems of illness and dying. Our God is the God of the living, not of the dead. The platonic ideas of afterlife no longer aid in finding the answers to the problems of life. Christ himself chose not to tell us about the state of our souls after death; death is not to be our concern. The needs of the living are our concern. Life must be embraced willingly by Christians. The sacraments of the sick must speak of God's love and of Christian acceptance of the ill and dying. To fail people in this, their time of need, is to fail in a basic task of any religion.

As the church uses fear of death to avoid preparing people for death, so does it use the fear of sex to avoid preparing people for marriage. Traditionally, the church has been firmly committed to monogamy: one man and one wife until the death of one of the partners. The sacrament of matrimony is both the inauguration and the symbol of that high standard. Yet it would be difficult for the church to come up with a theology of sex more at odds with its teaching on the permanence of marriage. This contradiction has become more apparent since the social sanctions and props have been pulled out from under permanent marriages. Now that the church no longer has the tools of social control at its disposal, it must completely re-examine its theology of sex if it is to uphold a Christian concept of marriage.

The New Testament teaches us that God, acting in the death and resurrection of Christ, has put all created powers at man's disposal: government, organization, science, physical power, and pleasure. Man has no longer any need to fear them, but to struggle with them, to humanize them, and bring them to serve his purposes. The victory of Christ robbed all of the forces of life of their demonic power to subdue man. Man is to share in this victory to the extent that he humanizes the world around him. The church exists to aid man in controlling the forces that brutalize the human spirit and decent instincts of men. One of the most dominant forces challenging man is his own sexuality. But armed with the confidence of faith, the Christian faces the challenge of sex not to suppress or exploit it, but as a means of carrying out his task of humanizing the world.

For centuries, the church has adhered to a platonic suspicion of pleasure. Sex has been considered as sin and love as an occasion of sin. Recently, the church has undone its condemnation of sex, but has rigorously tied down the goodness of sex to the biological function of reproduction. The idea that sexual pleasure itself could be a noble means to a noble end has not been officially accepted or taught. So far, the teaching and practice of the church continues on the basis that the legality of a valid marriage makes sex good; otherwise, it is bad. With such a negative approach to sex, the church thus disposes of one of the greatest tools for building up the permanence of family life. By placing a priority on the validity of the marriage and reserving choice sanctions for those who choose to disregard the church's conditions for that validity, the church almost renders impossible the development of those personal relationships necessary for a successful marriage.

By teaching that sex is either wrong or too sacred to enjoy outside marriage, the church forces people into marriage just to enjoy sex without guilt. By removing sex from the total complex of human experiences that are necessary for the development of satisfying relationships and stable marriages, we thereby place an importance upon it completely out of line with its actual value. Marriage is a practical arrangement of two people living together, an enterprise that demands skills in many areas, among which sex is definitely not the most important. Yet, by taking sex out of context before marriage, we make it often most difficult for people to put it into context after marriage. Under the present discipline, young people approach the choice of a mate—perhaps one of the most critical choices of life—with not much more than admonitions to stay pure and comply with the regulations of the church. Fasting and table etiquette may be helpful disciplines, but by themselves do not lead to good habits of health and nutrition.

Neither can we expect young people to approach marriage responsibly without knowing the place of sex in the total range of growth and responsibility.

It is not the job of the church to promote sex any more than to forbid it. But it is the job of the church to promote the Christian institution of marriage and develop the personal skills necessary for it. But the present discipline makes it often impossible to carry out that job. How can we teach responsibility in matters that are outlawed by the church? We have subverted the order of Christian morality here by putting written law above the demands of conscience, which is the final norm of Christian behavior. Compliance with the law does not make sex fully human, but love and responsibility do. Not that law and discipline are not helpful and necessary; but they are not absolute. For the Christian, the final rule for sexual morality—as for all other areas of conduct—is individual need and human happiness.

The church's exemption of sexual conduct from the normal rule of Christian ethics is based upon its rigid adherence to the natural law theory. As useful as this theory—borrowed from Stoic philosophy—may have been in the past to support the Christian institution of marriage, it has now been widely rejected outside the Roman Church. Instead of being an aid in the defense of the Christian faith, it has become an obstacle to it. Modern philosophy, as seen by many people, completely rejects the notion that man can arrive at the knowledge of the intrinsic purpose and nature of a thing through a rational process. Even more, the objective nature of knowledge itself is questioned. People refuse to accept any human proposition as absolute. Truth is whatever answers real human needs and is therefore relative to those needs. As a result of this change of attitudes, we have the anomaly of a religious group dictating to the rest of the world what is or is not "natural" rather than effectively conveying what has been revealed to it.

In giving moral leadership to the world, the church must take its cue from the world, see the hand of God in the moral progress of secular society, and preach the gospel in terms of what is good in the sight of all men. It is not the place of the church to demand allegiance to philosophical propositions that have been rationally deduced. This is nothing less than presenting as doctrine the teachings of men. Natural law theory is perhaps the greatest stumbling block we have unnecessarily placed in our brother's way. It should be rapidly removed so that like Paul we become all things to all men that we may be made partakers of the gospel of God's love.

By avoiding the real issue of practice and skill in human relationships—which alone can pull through a marriage today—the church leaves the impression that either its legal sanctions or sex itself, allowed within a valid marriage, will suffice for success. It is rarely admitted that sex, like everything else human, can be used as a means of withdrawal, rejection, or personal exploitation—within marriage as well as outside it. It is not permitted yet to say that sex, like all other pleasure, has been given man for the development of the human values of love and dedication. The church should exist to promote love, not inhibit it. The continued priority given to the legal conditions and sanctions for a valid marriage do not serve the purposes of the Christian love-ethic. On the contrary, it creates tragic marriages. What God hath joined is not always a valid marriage; neither is a valid marriage always joined by God.

The sacrament of marriage should point to the church's responsibility to develop the skills of personal relationships. The most difficult battle of life is communication, speaking honestly to one another. This is the most human and indispensable challenge we have to face. But how great it is! Nothing threatens us so much as the communication of ourselves. As soon as one speaks, he exposes himself to the possibility of rejection and ridicule. His most sensitive insights and precious convictions lie bare before the gaze of others. Yet self-communication is the only means of developing human life. The most urgent demand of human development is to trust others enough to entrust them with one's thoughts, to accept the response, and to listen to others honestly. This art demands great practice, training, support, and conviction. This most human of all skills is not provided by nature but needs to be acquired through imagination and labor. People constantly need to be encouraged to speak honestly if they are not to destroy themselves and others. The only dangerous ideas are the unspoken ones.

So demanding is the need for communication, people are always on the lookout for less demanding occupations. The church's teaching on sex often provides them with an out. The struggle for self-communication is often abandoned in favor of a quixotic conquest of sex, either in the form of personal domination or of ascetical rejection of others. The evil of sex provides a ready excuse to avoid the need for personal involvement, a handy scapegoat onto which all of one's problems can be projected. The sexual taboos taught in religion classes suddenly become bludgeons to use against one's spouse. The fear of sex which accompanies the legalistic approach to marriage gives ample support to an isolated God-and-me spirituality that leaves out the needs of others as well as one's own need for communication. No need to be the brother's keeper—it might involve sex, and that's bad. Or: no need to be the brother's keeper—it might involve something *besides* sex, and that's bad too. Thus partners in marriage utilize negative doctrines of sex to reject one another. One believes that sex is dirty; the other believes that there are no restrictions on sex within a valid marriage. Neither one has been taught to accept the responsibilities of love and communication.

The latest trend in the church's promotion of sexual fear is the attempt of popular theologians and liturgists to sacramentalize sex. They hope to justify the church's legalistic policies for marriage by making the sexual act something sacred and mystical, an occasion of grace. With sex regarded as something supernatural, they hope that it will not be so easily tampered with. They tend to forget that it is the lifelong institution of marriage that is the sacrament, not the individual sexual act. The Christian gospel gives all men the right to employ sex as human need indicates. Sex must be demythologized of both secular and religious myths before it can be coped with in a rational and human manner. A fear of the sacredness of sex is no better than a fear of its evil.

What are the obstacles blocking training in personal relationships in the church? Perhaps the enforced celibacy of the clergy and religious is one. Do the clergy and religious teachers possess enough openness and personal freedom to be able to inspire these qualities in others? Legalism and regimentation are other obstacles to communication. Salvation by adherence to external regulations militates against the risk and creativity demanded by personal relationships. The greatest obstacle to successful marriages is the breakdown of religious education for adults. Success in marriage does not come with knowing the church's doctrine on sex and complying with the legal forms. It comes with discipline and experience involved in developing satisfying relationships.

At a time when young people need guidance the most, the church seems to abandon them. Few Catholic young adults receive education in choosing a mate. Fewer still receive any assistance or guidance in adjusting during the first years of marriage. Group workshops in marriage for the difficult readjustment years of middle age are practically nonexistent. While we are tempted to smile at the thought of marriage difficulties in later years, the incidence of unhappiness developing then would justify the development of programs of counsel for the elderly. Each age, each year has its particular challenge. More than ever before, a marriage has to be re-created each year by the parties themselves. The freedom of our society and the lack of social sanctions against remarriage presents a great opportunity for the church in promoting personal fulfillment and responsibility. But the goal of monogamy demands a general overhaul of the church's attitude toward religious education.

If the church is really interested in reducing promiscuity, teen marriages, broken families, unhappy homes, and divorce, it must stop exploiting sexual fear for the purposes of social control. Its task is to build up in the individual, the family, and the community warm relationships by teaching people how to get along *with* one another, not *without* one another. The interpersonal demands of the Christian ethic must be preferred to a slavish insistence on legal validity. The goal of sexual education should be authentic and God-joined marriages, not just valid ones.

Once personal growth and relationships are taken as the primary end of marriage, then sex will be brought back into a Christian frame of reference. As all other forms of pleasure, it will be subordinate to the love-ethic instead of the law-ethic. Such an advance will provide the solution to birth control and eliminate one of the great disintegrating forces of marriage, fear of unwanted children. Such an advance of the church will greatly benefit the ethical progress of all men. It would enable marriage partners to attain much deeper relationships with others as well as with one another. Nothing creates openness and responsibility like freedom. The ability to choose the time of conception does not take this prerogative out of the hands of God, but merely gives man a greater share in God's responsibility. Our past acceptance of every hardship as the will of God gave very little credit to God's love or man's intelligence. It promoted a subhuman dependence on the caprice of nature. God demands that man take nature under control for the service of man. And what does it profit a man to gain control over the whole world if he does not control his own body?

The sexual preoccupation of our society is but a symptom of the coldness of hearts. The extreme legalism of the church's attitude toward sex does little to warm them up. The way to bring warmth into the world is not to condemn sex but to promote love. Racial injustice, indifference to poverty, acceptance of nuclear war, the isolation of persons and groups from one another, and the refusal to get involved are results of the church's failure to promote personal and physical affection. It is not sexuality that is wrecking the world, but man's refusal to love.

The concept of *orders* is something that properly belongs to the whole Christian people. Every Christian receives holy orders at baptism and is stationed on the front line of battle with the forces of evil. The common acceptance of orders as something restricted to the clergy no doubt springs from the days when the clerical church was considered a separate and private society. But in today's world, the opposition is not between lay society and ecclesiastical society but between the church and the world. This new frame of reference gives a completely different role to the ministry; it is no longer conceived as set over against the lay Christian, but with him. We have yet to attain an appreciation of the whole church, lay and clerical, not set over and against the rest of the world, but with it and for it.

The new perspective lends a much more functional purpose to holy orders—that of authority governing society. The Protestant Reformation seemed to force the church into overemphasizing the sacramental character of the priesthood in order to justify the legalistic excesses which were still identified with the essential make-up of the church. But the role of priests and bishops as the authorities within the church, a functional *part* of the church performing a necessary service to the rest of the body, is much more in keeping with the history and theology of the Bible. The clergy and the hierarchy are simply the leaders and professional workers of the church.

The existence of a body of professional church workers distinct from the main body of believers goes back to the Old Testament. Moses singled out the tribe of Levi to perform the office of priests in the temple. There later grew up separate classes of archivists, lawyers, and teachers. Christ combined the religious functions of these groups in his own person and in the role he gave to the apostles. The hierarchy was to be the teachers and leaders of the Christian church. These roles most accurately describe to the modern mind what Christ intended the apostles to be.

The dusty crew Christ gathered around him was the beginning of the clerical-religious complex of the Catholic Church. It was soon enlarged by the addition of presbyters and deacons. Later on, the religious communities of men and women that sprung up were incorporated into the professional ranks of the church. This special body of workers were dedicated to the work of the *rest* of the church, not taken *from* it but given *to* it, to serve its purposes. This is clearly stated by Paul: "And he himself gave some men as apostles, and some as prophets, others again as evangelists, and others as pastors and teachers, in order to perfect the saints for a work of ministry, for building up the body of Christ." (EPHESIANS 4:11–12.) The body of the faithful is consecrated to the work of ministry; the clergy is to aid them in that task by effective leadership.

During the Middle Ages, Old Testament concepts of priests and kings were applied to the clergy. With the onslaught of the Protestant Reformation, these concepts were defended by a metaphysical explanation of the concepts of sacrifice, sacrament, and juridical power. One of the greatest challenges facing the church is to divest itself of its claim to *coercive* jurisdiction, a claim totally out of keeping with the teaching of the New Testament. Only when the church rejects its compulsive idea of authority will it be able to exercise its authority effectively in the modern world. The leadership of the church was intended by Christ to be essentially a *teaching* leadership with the function of persuading other Christians to persuade the rest of men to know and obey God.

The effectiveness of the church's authority depends on its ability to win free assent and participation by members through persuasion instead of mere compliance through legal action. A prime requisite, it seems to me, is to guarantee more mobility and flexibility to the hierarchy and clergy itself. Nobody suffers more from the lack of freedom within the church than the clergy and hierarchy. The great majority of canonical regulations apply to them and not to the lay people. The present rigid structures make the church prey to certain classes and groups within a society and militate against the church's ministry to all men.

One solution would come in the recognition of a temporary priesthood. There is nothing in the Bible which justifies the extreme sanctions levied against priests who leave the ministry. Discussion has already begun on the possibility of ordaining priests for set periods of time and of discharging priests as utility or desire indicates. The dignity of the priesthood need not be permanently inherent in the person of the one ordained. The church has in its power to relieve priests of their ministry with honor and appreciation. Even within the traditional theory of the permanence of vows, there is room to allow for such dismissals.

Another obstacle to the effectiveness of authority is celibacy. This often repels the best leadership types from the church instead of attracting them to it. Celibacy can be a great aid to the ministry, but its effectiveness demands that it be voluntary. The whole evangelical meaning of celibacy is the freedom it gives for dedication to the people. But the present discipline exploits celibacy as a means of social control, not freedom. Subdeacons are required to bind themselves to celibacy after they have spent up to twelve years in preparation for the priesthood. With this amount of investment behind them, the freedom of their sacrifice can be questioned. The relinquishment of the right to raise a family is quite a commitment to the demands of the company, one that does not tend to promote creative nonconformity. So prominent is the element of celibacy that it is largely identified with the priesthood itself, a fact that contributes little to leadership. A priest's identification with his priestly career quite often becomes a matter of personal security within the organizational church rather than a matter of professional dedication to the work at hand. This does not speak well of Christian freedom or responsibility.

A third obstacle to effective leadership is the poor training of priests. Already there is much discussion about moving seminaries back to the city where seminarians can take courses in local universities. If the church is to be in the world, it is essential that priests be educated within the main stream of its intellectual life. Until the seminaries are established on the campuses of secular colleges, much can be done to open up the seminaries for academic freedom. Outside lecturers and teachers can be brought to the seminary for courses. Seminary courses can be drastically shortened to allow more study at outside institutions. The classroom and lecture situation within the seminary can be modified to allow for more informal and effective methods of learning. The scholastic rating of seminaries can be elevated through greater demand for excellence in teachers and textbooks. And, finally, more freedom can be given seminarians for off-campus experience and training in hospitals, schools, colleges, and religious and social centers. The only way to make missionaries out of men is to let them *be* missionaries. I believe that the greater demands for more clergy and a better trained one are not to be met by building more seminaries, but by making more efficient use of existing ones and of outside facilities.

Authority and citizenship depend on one another. There is no justification for hoping that the laity will develop an aggressive independence in their witness without radical changes in the organization of the clergy. Any means of bringing the clergy closer to the lives of the people, away from the isolated enclosures of the rectory, will not destroy their effectiveness as leaders but only strengthen it. To the extent that freedom of authority is enhanced in the clergy, the lay people will attain freedom to witness. The sacrament of Holy Orders involves the whole church. Authority and power are not metaphysical elements contained in the clergy; they are moral realities made of the relationships existing between leaders and the rest of the community. Their effectiveness depends upon the active contributions of the whole community, upon the conversation that takes place both horizontally and vertically. When the priests are in contact with the people, when the fraternal nature of authority displaces paternal domination, when persuasion replaces dictation, and when self-determination is valued more than mere conformity, then authority becomes leadership.

CHAPTER SEVEN

The Democratic Church

The freedom of the Christian has become a popular topic among Catholic writers today. Seen in both a theological and contemporary aspect, freedom is the choice product of God's labor in the world. And yet in spite of the new awareness of this gift of freedom, we see little sign of its acceptance in the official life of the church; freedom is not yet guaranteed and made a part of the institutional life of the church. This reluctance is based on a dilemma that we must now face: How can the freedoms we enjoy in a democratic society possibly be transferred to the church with its divinely established hierarchy? The Christians' great freedom in a democratic world becomes a stumbling block in his church life. Engaged in the great variety of activities, interests, and organizations necessary for the growth of democracy, he finds his responsibilities in the church are limited merely to carrying out the demands of his immediate superior. This limitation militates against individual initiative, unauthorized activity, and nonconformity. How can the need for obedience and the familial trust that should characterize the Christian community be reconciled with the need for freedom and self-determination? And more, how can this freedom become a part of the institutional church?

Democratic institutions have done much in secular life to reconcile the need for authority and freedom. Can it provide the same solution for the church? Is democracy, first of all, a theological possibility for the church's own institutions? This chapter is an attempt to answer that question on the theoretical level and to suggest some practical applications. The next chapter will explore the serious juridical inadequacies of church law and possible solutions. Further studies will have to be done on the traditional forms of ecclesiastical government of the past in order to determine what structures, if any, are essential to the nature of the church, and what was borrowed from the political make-up of succeeding generations. Sociological studies can show us what the present power structure of the church is, as opposed to the theory of church structure as contained in dogma and canon law. From there the church will have to decide what can and should be changed in order that the organization patterns of the church effectively advance its work and concerns. At present, it seems to many that the present organization of the church hinders the fulfillment of its tasks.

The often-heard phrase, "The church is not a democracy!" is a mild understatement. Our problem now is to find out whether or not it could be a democracy. First of all, we should know what we are talking about when we speak of a democracy; next we should examine the nature of authority in the church. Finally we can speculate on the application of democracy to the needs of the church. We begin by presuming that the reasons for the undemocratic church are not only historical, but also theoretical. Our object is to examine the objections to democratic structures in the church and weigh their validity.

The first objection to democracy in the church is that sovereignty in the Christian community has been given directly by God to the hierarchy. And since democracy is allegedly based on the idea that sovereignty rests directly and solely in the people and they are the ones who confer it on some delegated persons who then act as their agents in running the government, we say that sovereignty is exercised by the ruling power with the consent of the governed. When those who rule fail to conform to the wishes of the people, they are put out of office. This procedure and the philosophy that underlies it is incompatible with the nature of the church. Hence democracy has no place in the church.

True, democracy thus conceived may have no place in the church. But while this conception of democracy is still prevalent, it has long been discredited by political scientists as a realistic explanation of what happens between rulers and the governed in a democratic society. One college text states:

> With the wealth of historical material now at hand, we can definitely say that the social contract theory was an imaginative rationalization for eighteenth century social and political trends. Because the advocates of these various theories on the origin of the state were not restricted by the facts which modern research has presented, they could allow their fancies full play, held in check only by the limits of their own imaginations (Robert Wallace Brewster, *Government in Modern Society*. Boston: Houghton Mifflin Company, 1958; 619 pp. P. 31.).

The social scientists today attempt to be realistic: in democratic governments, those in ruling positions exercise *real,* not delegated, sovereignty. Society does not seem able not to have some special ruling group. A sovereign of some type seems to be a necessary and organic part of any society. The problem of the source of this sovereignty is a false problem. It is like discussing the source of the authority of the brain over the rest of the body. Wherever you have a living organism made up of disparate units and a variety of functions, all united by a common goal, you must have a centralized system of demand and response. The theory that the power of ruling authority depends upon a prior contract, or even a prior consent of the people, rests on the impossible supposition that a society could refuse any consent and still remain a society.

In human society, people are *always* giving allegiance to some special person or group of persons whose authority is constituted not by some previous agreement or consent, even implied, but by the very obedience of the people. The reception of their obedience does not make the rulers agents of their authority, but rather *rulers who are obeyed.* Obedience and authority are correlative elements that bring one another into existence. So great is the need for authority and obedience in society, that we never have a society existing without them. God's intention in nature could hardly be more evident.

Since the church is monarchical by divine institution, it has no place for democratic structures. This second argument opposing democracy in the church is based upon the distinction between types of government: those governed by the one, by the few, and by the many—monarchy, oligarchy, and democracy. But there is a tendency to pretend that governments exist in pure forms, that all decisions are made identically, either by one, by a few, or by the many. Such instances would be extremely rare. History shows that most governments contain elements of each of these classifications; they are made up of mixtures, in varying degrees, of these types. When we speak of democratic governments as opposed to totalitarian governments, we are concerned with the degree of one element or another that prevails in a state. A pure democracy is hard to find. But we can say that a government is democratic *insofar* as the great mass of people exercise an effective role in the decisions that make up the work of government.

A third objection follows from the others: control or restraint placed upon sovereignty destroys sovereignty, since the restraining influence is the more powerful. Since Christ gave sovereignty directly to the hierarchy and not to the laity, there is no possibility of the laity exercising restraint or control over this sovereignty. This same objection once opposed the Federal Constitution and now opposes the United Nations: sovereignty that is limited is no sovereignty at all.

Several errors lie behind this thinking. The first arises from a metaphysical approach that conceives power as a *thing* that is able to be possessed and lost. It is rather a moral reality that depends upon the interpersonal relationships and reactions between the sovereign and the governed. Power *does* reside in the sovereign, but his "possession" of it depends on the acquiescence of the governed. It depends, actually, more on them than on him. The power of authority is built from the bottom up, not from the top down. Whether it is fear, ignorance, or reason that motivates obedience, it is obedience that creates sovereignty.

Secondly, to say that sovereignty is unlimited is to say that it is not responsible to the needs of the community; an unlimited sovereign would be able to act in any arbitrary manner and to be obeyed absolutely. An unlimited sovereign evidently would not be for the good of the community since he could violate the dictates of reason in demanding obedience to the ridiculous and immoral.

Common sense and history show us that sovereignty is always limited by that which the subjects will in fact obey. "Is sovereignty limited or unlimited?" means in practice, "Will the people absolutely obey anything that the sovereign orders?" The argument that sovereignty is unlimited comes down to the statement that we must either obey in everything or we will not obey at all.

The next problem is how to keep the exercise of sovereignty confined to the dictates of reason. How do we check the abuse of authority? We can look to civil society for some answers, since civil society is decidedly authoritarian. It should be evident that democracy is not antiauthoritarian or even antihierarchical. In our own democracy we daily submit to very authoritarian decisions by different agencies of government, as well as to such decisions made in the field of education, commerce, and so on. The political scientist Carl J. Friedrich confirms the fact that the authoritarian nature of civil society resembles in many ways the structure of the church; he then goes on to say:

> Even so general a statement shows that the semi-military, authoritarian nature of a government service is by no means a gratuitous invention of petty autocrats, but inherent in the very nature of process which form the essence of all administrative services. This point hardly requires emphasizing in an age which exhibits examples of this same authoritarian, hierarchical control on all sides, since large-scale business corporations, trade unions and many other organizations are conducted on this pattern (*Constitutional Government and Democracy*. Boston: Blaisdell Publishing Company, 1950. P. 47.).

It can be claimed that nowhere is civil authority more respected than in a democracy. There are many reasons for this. The *function* of authority in relation to the life of the community is more clearly defined. Society has divested political authority of much of its mythical and divine elements which once attributed to rulers a purpose not found in society itself, and which once justified the neglect, caprice, and cruelty of official actions.

Democratic processes serve to protect authority from both corruption and neglect of responsibility. No longer shielded from the view of the rest of men by recourse to a divine right to privacy, the public official is held accountable to the public for all his words, actions, and policies that have bearing on his field of public responsibility. Thomas Paine wrote in *The Rights of Man:* "In the representative government, the reason for everything must publically appear. Every man is a proprietor in government, and considers it a necessary part of his business to understand." Democratic processes also serve to keep the rulers more informed of the needs of society, more threatened, to be sure, to take the necessary steps to know the facts and the feelings of their constituencies. Familiarity with the factual situation is the *sine qua non* of effective government.

The ease with which allegiance is transferred from one government to another, under due process and without any violence or defection, creates great continuity and stability in a democracy. No matter how unpopular a leader might become, the people can stay and wait until the next election, during which time the leader may choose to redeem himself or finally lose office. The great complexity of democratic processes themselves have a great educative value both for the people and for the authorities. In a free society, needs are complex and solutions are harder to come by. But open channels of communication and participation in government by the people give great strength and flexibility to authority: it is more able to reconcile widely different interests and bring some satisfaction to all elements in society. It is also able to rapidly meet and adapt to new and unexpected challenges without a breakdown of law and established procedures. It moves with the people as it leads them.

In all of this we can say that the basic difference between democratic and nondemocratic governments is that in a democracy *authority is made accountable to society* for its actions by means of the democratic processes. This happens in much the same way that a person is made accountable to society for his actions as a private individual through the processes of law, law enforcement, and the courts. In both cases, the private individual and the political figure are directly responsible to God for the morality of their actions. In both cases, these structures, different for each, support and develop their responsibilities. In both cases, the freedom of the individual is not hindered but guaranteed and protected by those social structures. Democratic institutions—the vote, a free press, set terms of office, an independent judiciary, bicameral legislatures, and so forth—do for authority what law does for the private individual.

We can now turn to the problem of the church: Does the

divine institution of the church allow for democratic processes that serve to make authority accountable to the rest of the community for its actions? Is ecclesiastical authority accountable only to God or did the intention of Christ allow for the human correction and prevention of the abuse of authority in the church? Considering the totally human situation of the church, we feel that democratic structures have a place in the church. This conclusion comes from 1) the *fraternal* nature of authority as expounded in the New Testament, 2) the relative success of democratic experience in dealing with abuse of authority, and 3) the discoveries of modern research and political science regarding the nature and exercise of authority.

As Catholics we are very much aware of the authority given to Simon Peter in MATTHEW 16 and JOHN 21. We are continually taught of the authoritarian nature of the church. And yet we rarely have recourse to the many other texts that deal with the nature and exercise of that authority. We do not revert to those texts that speak of the freedom of the individual that is given by God to those who love him. In fact, a general reading of the Bible can easily leave us with the impression that it is anti-institutional and antipolitical, if not anti-authoritarian, because of its obvious emphasis on the rights and freedoms of the individual. Its general approach to human institutions can best be described as irreverent.

One of the most basic themes in the Bible teaches us that man attains his perfection and freedom in his submission to God's purposes. By articulating his response to God's demands, man is liberated from external pressures and consideration. A spiritual man, wrote Paul, is above even the law; he possesses the freedom of a son of God because he has been given the good Spirit who informs him of the inner meaning of the law which is love.

But the seemingly anti-authoritarian conclusions of this

doctrine can be avoided if we briefly review the political situations in which revelation took place.

In the Old Testament, people were aware of government and authority as something especially harsh and oppressive. It was natural to think of salvation in terms of release from this oppression. Among the Hebrews, God was known as the living God who acted in freedom and whose actions bestowed freedom. All human kings were considered as rivals to God, the only king worth serving. The doctrine of God's kingship and his kingdom were taught by contrasting them to the rule of pagan kings.

During the wanderings of the Israelites in the desert, God had his people all to himself and they became aware of the directness of their relationship to him. After the occupation of Canaan, however, they became aware also of their existence as a *people* and felt a need for a human king such as other nations had.

This was first interpreted as a weakening of their faith, and God revealed his disappointment to the prophet Samuel: "Listen to the voice of the people according to all that they say to you; for they have not rejected you, but they have rejected me from being king over them." (I SAMUEL 8:7.) But soon the idea of a temporal government became reconciled with the kingship of Yahweh.

The king of Israel was to be like no other king on earth. His power to rule was limited by God's word. He was not an absolute sovereign, but was regarded instead as God's servant and had to obey as well as enforce God's law. Protected too was the freedom of the prophets to openly criticize and accuse the king of abuses. Here we already have a division of power. As G. Ernest Wright points out, "The government was thus a constitutional monarchy, and the basic freedoms of the people were protected by God against the encroachments of royal power" (G. Ernest Wright and Reginald H. Fuller, *The Book of the Acts of God.* P. 116.).

The security and justice which had been hoped for by the people were provided only for a short period of about a hundred years under the kings. Only King David ever seemed to measure up to the standards demanded by God. He was later to be regarded as the ideal leader, meek and concerned with the establishment of justice: "And he chose David, his servant, and took him from the sheepfolds; from following the ewes he brought him to shepherd Jacob, his people, and Israel, his inheritance." (PSALMS 78:70–71.)

The remaining history of the kings of Israel has aptly been described as God's controversy with the kings. Because of their defection and the unfaithfulness of the people, God used the events of international history to judge his people until finally they were swallowed up by the empires. God's judgment found expression in the records of Isaiah: "My watchmen are blind, all of them unaware. . . . They are relentless dogs, they know not when they have enough. These are the shepherds who know no discretion; each of them goes his own way, every one of them to his own gain." (ISAIAH 56:10–11.) The people's disillusionment with any prospect of freedom under an earthly ruler grew into a hope of some supernatural intervention of God that would establish a new kingdom under God's appointed servant: "Woe to the shepherds who mislead and scatter the flock of my pasture, says the LORD. Behold the days are coming, says the LORD, when I will raise up a righteous shoot to David; as king he shall reign and govern wisely, he shall do what is just and right in the land." (JEREMIAH 23:1, 5.) This new king would rule with truth, mercy, and suffering.

In fulfilling the hopes of the Old Testament, Christ completed its teaching by pointing up the limitations of human authority made by the authority of God. Obedience to human law is contingent upon the absolute loyalty we owe to God:

"And why do you transgress the commandment of God because of your tradition? Hypocrites, well did Isaiah prophesy of you saying, 'This people honors me with their lips, but their heart is far from me; and in vain do they worship me, teaching as doctrine the precepts of men.'" MATTHEW 15:3, 7-9.

"How can you believe who receive glory from another, and do not seek the glory which is from the only God?" JOHN 5:44.

"But woe to you Pharisees! because you pay tithes on mint and rue and every herb, and disregard justice and the love of God." LUKE 11:42.

Christ himself was well known for his sense of freedom and independence from human respect in his obedience to God: "Master, you are an honest man, we know; you teach in all honesty the way of life that God requires, truckling to no man, whoever he may be." (MATTHEW 22:16.) So keen was he to distinguish between human and divine authority that he charged, "Why do you call me good? No one is good except God alone." (LUKE 18:19.) And he demanded this same freedom from human concern in his followers: "If anyone comes to me and does not hate his father and mother and wife and children and brothers and sisters, yes, and even his own life, he cannot be my disciple." (LUKE 14:26.)

As much as Christ insisted on the direct relationship between the members of the kingdom and God, he nevertheless provided for human authority in the church he founded. This is most evident in the abundant texts in which he counsels the apostles on the exercise of their authority:

"You know that the rulers of the gentiles lord it over them, and their great men exercise authority over them. Not so is it among you. On the contrary, whoever wishes to become great among you shall be your slave; even as the Son of Man has not come to be served but to serve, and to give his life as a ransom for many." MATTHEW 20:25-28.

"But do not you be called 'Rabbi' for one is your Master and you are all brothers. And call no one on earth your father; for one is your Father, who is in heaven. Neither be called masters;

for one only is your Master, the Christ. He whoever exalts himself shall be humbled, and whoever humbles himself shall be exalted." MATTHEW 23:8–12.

The example of the Good Shepherd, who intimately knows the individual needs of his sheep, is to be the pattern of authority exercised in the church. The bishop and his flock are to be as open and direct with one another as are the Father and the Son.

The apostles understood both the scope and the limitations of their authority. In his letters, Paul was ever conscious of the freedom and dignity of the members of the church and was most honest with himself in the matter of his own authority. As God's fellow-laborer, he was the servant of God's people: "For we preach not ourselves, but Jesus Christ as Lord, and ourselves merely as your servants in Jesus." (II CORINTHIANS 4:5.) The first pope exhorted the presbyters: "Tend the flock of God which is among you, governing not under constraint, but willingly, according to God; nor yet for the sake of base gain, but eagerly; nor yet as lording it over your charges, but becoming from the heart a pattern to the flock." (I PETER 5:2–3.)

The New Testament closed with the political structures of the church potentially developed, with a society that was aware of its allegiance to its leaders and those leaders keenly aware of the extent of their responsibilities.

The political life of the church remained only potentially developed until the beginning of canon law with the decrees of the Council of Nicea in 325. Here a remarkable transference began to take place within the church: the absorption of Roman law. Just as Constantine saw the usefulness of Christianity for the unity of the empire, so the church employed the structures of Roman law to embody its own social awareness of itself. And not only did it borrow the outward form and political organization from Roman law, but also Roman ideology. And so today we have not only the terms *diocese* and *parish* but also *authority, tradition,* and *religion*—borrowed from and found deep in Roman history.

The word *authority* derives from the verb "to augment," which tells us that all political life is founded on that which supports and augments the sacred action that founded the city of Rome. To be engaged in politics, for a Roman, meant to preserve the founding of the city and the values embodied by that founding. The authority was always derivative and dependent upon the fidelity to the intention of the founders (*auctores*) of the city. The elders (*patres*) and the senators were endowed with this authority by descent or transmission (*traditio*) from those who had laid the foundation for all things to come. The official cult of the gods was, according to Roman interpretation, the bond (*religio*) that held the citizen close to those ancient events. The authenticity and validity of all political life was supported by this Roman trinity of authority, tradition, and religion. Nothing was authentic unless it was marked with the *auctoritas maiorum,* the precedent of tradition. The criteria for authenticity hearkened not to the needs of the people so much as to the interpretation of the past.

The transferal of the tradition-bound Roman legal system to the church was due in great measure to the writings of Augustine, whom Hannah Arendt calls "the only great philosopher the Romans ever had," since he gave a philosophical expression to their political experience. Whatever we might think now about the Romanization of the church, it could hardly be questioned at the time. With the invasion of the barbarians, the salvation which the church could offer the world was symbolized in the appeal to Roman law and order in contrast to the chaos of the times. No one can doubt that the Roman spirit served the church well.

The change in this political philosophy came with the development of science and knowledge. The idea of authority changed along with the concepts of "truth," "knowledge," and "rights." The radical change in the concept of truth that came with the development of experimental science brought a change in the concept of society and individual freedom. Until the time of Galileo, mankind operated on a somewhat materialistic idea of knowledge which consisted in the appropriation of the truths handed down from the ancients and upon which all subsequent truths were to be added. The scientific revolution was only possible when men freed themselves from the obligation of fitting new observations into the systems of the past and began looking into each phenomenon with a fresh and noncommitted approach. One theologian remarks concerning this intellectual revolution:

> As Kant quite correctly remarked in the *Preface* to the second edition of his *Critique of Pure Reason,* science did not make any serious progress until Galileo had the happy thought of subjecting the world to a methodical enquiry instead of being satisfied with gathering facts "like a schoolboy who lets himself be told whatever pleases his master." Since Galileo, the man of science turns to nature "as a presiding judge who forces the witnesses to reply to the questions he asks." He anticipates nature with logical structures erected by his intelligence, with hypotheses of his own free invention, and above all with a mathematical system of axioms fashioned by himself. Scientific truth is not a copy of an image passively received, but the fruit of a laborious and endless dialogue between thought and reality (Albert Dondeyne, "Truth and Freedom. A Philosophical Study," in *Truth and Freedom.* Pittsburgh: Duquesne University Press, 1955; 133 pp. P. 37.).

This new awareness of man's relationship to reality brought a corresponding change in man's approach to society itself. No longer bound by the systems of the past, man became more free to examine the dynamics of society in themselves. From the old notion that truth was a system to which anything new must conform came the obligation of the individual to work out his lot in the station of life to which he was born on the assumption that he was divinely ordained or called to this destiny. But once truth was no longer viewed as something known once and for all and knowledge as something that never changes, the field of man's knowledge of himself and his environment became open to investigation and patterns of society open to criticism and change. The recognition that truth is something to be pursued rather than possessed brought the conviction that present political structures don't have to be so.

In this new atmosphere, man felt free to reconstruct society in such a way as to take care of not only his material needs and his need for security and stability, but also his more characteristic need for freedom: the desire to experience new and emergent value-satisfactions. Society, men began to think, can be organized in accordance with present needs, not a pre-established pattern, in order that men can create some sort of identity for themselves as human persons. This basic need to become somebody and to be acknowledged as having importance is most characteristically satisfied in what we call a free society.

This need for individual self-determination and initiative was often confirmed by spokesmen within the church such as Cardinal Mercier:

> Detest this slogan: "One must act like everybody else." On the contrary, everyone must act differently from the others, for everyone is a personality whose aim it is to lead a full life and reach complete self-development. The spineless laziness of the masses springs from the fact that so few people have the courage to examine themselves and discover what they are capable of becoming and decide that they want to become it (*Oeuvres pastorales*, Vol. I, Louvain, 1929, p. 429, as quoted in Louis de Raeymaeker, "Truth and Freedom of Scientific Research According to Cardinal Mercier," in *Truth and Freedom*, P. 24.).

The events of history seem to indicate that the structures of the church have been derived from secular society in the past. The church is always in relation to the world, so are its political structures, its political philosophy, and the meaning it attaches to authority and obedience. These realities can only be defined in terms of the language of the times if they are to be defined at all. The church cannot express its basic message to the world in terms of a political philosophy of a past age. It would seem that democratic processes are not intrinsically opposed to the nature of the church. Democracy is able to guarantee both the effectiveness of authority and the freedom of the individual. Through democratic structures, not only are the absolute powers of authority eliminated and brought more in line with reason, but the function of government itself is both clarified and supported. The changes of government necessary to accommodate to the changing needs of society are carried out by due process without revolution and mass defection. Such an arrangement calls for an incalculable amount of labor on the part of both rulers and citizens. Society is never fully established. It is always in the making; so is liberty, and so is authority.

But another question now arises: Can the reform of the church so ardently desired by all be accomplished without democratic reforms? We can all easily criticize church prelates, complain about the lack of free speech and free assembly, bewail the church's scandalous inertia to meet social problems and the one-hundred-year intellectual gap between the church and the world. But can such defects be remedied without drastic changes in the church's political life? Social and juridical structures themselves communicate a message and educate; they influence our ideas and life more than we care to admit. The modern social teachings of the church bear this out: social patterns and structures determine the welfare of men and are *perfectible*. Is the church really exempt from the dynamics of social life or are not the problems facing the church a result of misunderstanding and misapplying those dynamics? Does not the social doctrine of the church apply to the church itself as a society?

We often hear the claim that decentralization is the answer to the political reform of the church. But why should the church become decentralized just when mankind is coming to appreciate its own solidarity? More than ever there is need of a strong executive power in the church, one that is able to overcome the forces that resist reform and reunion. What is more, reforms are needed on the local level as well. A pastor of a small town can be as remote from the real needs of his people as the bishop or the Roman Curia. There is more need for efficiency on every level of church government, but this efficiency can be obtained only through procedures of communication and control. The problems of the church cannot be solved merely by passing them on down to a lower jurisdiction; problems must be met on the levels at which they can be effectively handled.

The problem of the responsibility of the layman will hardly be solved without giving him the freedom to participate on every level of church government. We can hardly expect a man to do his best *for* an organization unless he is given a share of freedom to operate *within* it. Church structures should manifest the fact that the layman is a subject of the church, not the object of it. They should speak of the belief in the presence of God's Spirit in man. Present structures conceal rather than reveal that fact. The modern mind perceives little of the presence of God's Spirit in church structures that symbolize a political system that was identified with the past and that smothered all personal initiative. Why should the church, with its doctrine of freedom, be so bound to these ancient Roman forms? Cannot the layman be as effectively protected in the exercise of his freedom within the church as well as within secular society?

Certainly there will be great problems of inefficiency and

complication once we begin to open up communications. But unearthing and facing the problems is the first step to progress. How many have left the church just because their own problems were not of serious concern to the church as such? The problems created by free expression, diversity of thought, and participation will not be as great as the problems we now face. But as free men, we can choose the type of problems we would like to face: the labor and delay involved in democratic discussion and leadership or the countless frustrations of unmet religious needs. Too often, the failure to exercise religious leadership and implement the religious inspirations of people have been excused on the basis of the church's ancient structures. If this is so, it is time to change those structures.

We can begin by educating ourselves to the responsibilities of freedom. The Bible teaches that the liberty that comes with obedience to God is in no way confined to the obedience we owe our human superiors. Their commands are only a small part of God's will. Conformity to rules is not the total scope of the virtue of obedience, may often be sinful, and usually can be improved upon by bringing it more in line with the needs of the situation.

The repetition of what others have done does not guarantee the authenticity of our actions or put us into the life-giving stream of Christian tradition. Somehow, we can train ourselves to become less dependent on regulations and more dependent on God's will coming to us in the needs of people as interpreted by the Bible. Our grasp of the truth of a situation may be fragmentary and transitional, but it must be acted upon.

We have to grow up in our political thinking by comparing what goes on in secular society with problems faced in the church. For too long we have patterned the relationship between clergy and laity on the prepolitical relationships between a master and slave, a parent and child, a shepherd and his sheep, or worse, between a benefactor and his beneficiary. Such relationships are not fitting between adults in a free society, especially in the church. The laity do not have to be the passive element of the church; neither do their responsibilities pertain just to giving money. They can be given full responsibilities as citizens of God's household, true subjects of his rule.

Democratic changes in the church are *urgently* needed. Political changes have been long overdue and the losses have been great. Further delay is but participation in the failures of the past. Let us openly petition that the proposed revision of canon law become a matter of universal concern and activity. This across-the-board review of the general legislation of the church will have a more lasting effect than the changes enacted by the Vatican Council. The only real reforms are structural ones. But a group of cardinals and canonical experts are hardly adequate for such a task, according to all the standards of political behavior. The cardinals, with all their good will and learning, are an interest group in themselves and are not adequate to legislate for other interest groups. It is a basic reality that interest groups are properly represented only by their own members. The doctrine of God's love for all his people dictates that the needs of all be properly attended to in the revision of church law. It should be the aim of the church to involve national conventions representing as complete a cross section of the church as possible to suggest and review legislation before enactment by the central administration.

There is need for immediate access to grievance machinery and court hearings for all church members. Freedoms of expression and assembly must be carefully defined and protected if the church is to evolve solutions for rapidly increasing problems. A great variety of theologies, liturgies, and programs need to be tolerated if the church is to be truly catholic. I envision a church that will be a homeland for religious freedom, in which there is room for high and low forms of worship, gospel singers and social gospelers, activists and passivists, people who are other-directed, book-centered, cult-centered, and antiliturgical—a church where a jazz Mass will be as authentic an expression of religious feeling as Palestrina.

Finally, we must have popular elections of prelates and popular selection of pastors. There can hardly be any restoration of freedom within the church without this form of direct contact between church people and their leaders. We can elect prelates for set terms of office. Or, as an alternative, elect them for life terms and have them delegate certain powers to elected officials. In this way the prelate could be a "head of state" exercising liturgical and diplomatic functions, but leaving the matters of executive administration in the hands of elected and trained technicians. In this way, also, prelates would be more free for the traditional tasks of teaching and preaching.

Our goal would certainly include the writing of a constitution for the church, one which clearly protects the rights of all by defining them and setting limits on the exercise of authority. There are enough precedents in civil government and the government of other churches from which to draw. There is also a great fund of knowledge available for this task in the political sciences.

The church is fully human. The dynamics of social relationships do obtain here, perhaps more fully than in other societies. And the political structure of this organization, as that of others, ought to be an expression of planned and reasoned relationships in accord with the concerns of the organization. Society is just that: relationships that are organized by determined human decisions and not by chance or nature. It will only be by the recognition of our ability to control, or be controlled by, the political structures of the church that effective internal reform can take place. This takes clearheaded planning and organization. There will be no substitute for heroism and great labor.

CHAPTER EIGHT

The Public Church

"The only thing wrong with the French Revolution was that it left the church untouched," a theologian once told me. As fortunate or unfortunate as this failure may have been, it is evidently true. The great political reforms inaugurated by the bloody event did not penetrate the church. In fact we may conclude that the French Revolution and the new political order it brought into the world only guaranteed the church's perpetuation of its ancient legal and political structures. In a free society, an authoritarian church is no longer a personal threat; one can just leave if he chooses, without any fear of reprisals. So that is exactly what has happened in the church on a grand scale over the last two-hundred years. The rebels and those not content with the lack of freedom within the church have just walked out. People have refused to be an enemy of the church; they have just turned their back on it. The People's Republic of East Germany waited for several years before it constructed the Berlin Wall. It was glad to get rid of the revolutionaries and the malcontents first. The Roman Church has waited and watched reformers leave the church for centuries now, much to its great relief—and loss.

But something strange has been happening these last few years. The reformers have decided that it does the church no good just to get out of it. They are choosing to stay and fight rather than switch. This is not so much the result of a particular affection for the church but of a particular affection for man. The church in its present form is seen more and more as a drag, a burden in fact, on the rest of the community. It is no longer smart to act as if the church just isn't there, or to tolerate it as a curious form of satisfaction for those who like that kind of thing. It is now considered too much as a threat to be ignored, even by its own sons.

The church is big and politically potent. It is aligned with the status quo and the wealthy, many of whom are big industrialists. It is still a closed society in which its internal policies are immune to reform from within and from without. In a secular society that is striving to be free and ethical, it is becoming more and more difficult to tolerate the petty autocracies that exist within public institutions. Principles of human dignity and freedom cannot be reserved just to a certain phase of secular government; they must permeate every phase of life, every business, every family, every club, and every organization. Whatever smacks of totalitarian imposition of one man's ideas upon another is a threat to a free society. This is why the church has come under attack—now from within.

It is amazing how churchmen have suddenly taken the political structures of the church seriously. At one time they held a very Machiavellian attitude toward church government: whatever works to serve the needs of the hierarchy is good. Clerical immunity still protects them in this attitude. Churchmen were slow to come to the revolutionary insights of the last two centuries: political structures and procedures are not indifferent to the demands of morality. Reform means legal reform, the replacement of bad laws with good laws, of unethical processes with ethical ones. Reform is always a matter of conversion from evil to good, not just a matter of modernizing equipment, establishing better public relations, or coming to grips with the modern world. If it is reform that we desire, the goal is not *aggiornamento,* a mere updating, but radical surgery in the political body of the church. Reforms are not won by committee evaluations and recommendations but by battles and wars of a political, if not military, nature.

Reform demands sacrifice, organization, strategy, courage, and great conflict. People in positions of privilege rarely consent to the change of law voluntarily. But the situation has to be changed so that they do consent voluntarily. New pressures need to be created that make it more uncomfortable for them not to consent than to consent. This must be done by those who seriously love the cause of reform and appreciate the urgency of its need. It is time for churchmen, both clergy and lay, to take their church seriously and to involve themselves in the battle of church reform. Freedom, especially within the church, never comes as a free gift, a kind of courtesy, from the top down. It must be won. If Catholics are upset with the programs offered by the local church, it is time for them to stop feeling disgruntled about it and do something to change the situation—something effective. Their parish is *their* church, it is the real church, the one in which their salvation will be won or lost. They can no longer feel that the real church is someplace else where things are better—Chicago, St. Louis, France, or the next diocese over. Chances are that things are about as bad in those places too for the same reasons: fear, apathy, and silence on the part of those who know things should be better but do not take up arms. Freedom is available, now, within the church, to all who want to pay the price for it.

But if we want a revolution (can there be reform without one?), we need a plan. We need specific grievances, first of all, and specific changes in laws we desire to remedy. Only we know what will protect our rights effectively in the church. Secondly, we need a strategy, which will not be taken up here. This is too much a matter of local concern to warrant any suggestions from outsiders; people generally know where their leaders are the most vulnerable.

But we do need a plan, goals to work for. What kind of a church do we want? This is determined by what we think the church should be doing. The task now is not to set up new programs of church activity, but to discover why those programs have not been set up all along. Our first task is not to make the church relevant to the needs of man, but to find out what has been keeping it from being relevant. We are not really in a position to be dictating new organizational patterns to the church; but we are in a position to secure the freedom necessary for organizational changes to take place. It is not ours to tell others in the church what they should be doing as Christians, but to secure the right for them to do as they see fit. The church already has an organizational structure; people are already doing things. It is our task to move from where we are, to work with the present systems of canon law, diocesan policies, and parish procedures in order to reconstruct a free church. What we need is not new programs but new procedures, procedures under which new programs can freely develop.

We first need a theology. It should be simply stated, in slogans perhaps. Here are some principles on which we can proceed:

1. *There must be no compulsion in religion.* Truth is its own best defense. The function of the Mosaic law in the Old Testament has now been taken over by secular governments. The government of the church must manifestly rest upon the love-ethic. Enforcement of its teachings must come from persuasion, not constraint or threat of sanction. The church, as every other organization in a free society, is *de facto* a voluntary organization. This situation demands that disciplinary procedures be limited strictly to administrative concerns, and then only under provision of the law.

2. *The church is a public institution.* Authority in the church is publicly accountable to the rest of the body of the church for all its official actions. Areas of secrecy are to be strictly provided for and regulated by law. The day is gone when the church was thought of as a piece of private prop-

erty belonging to the hierarchy. Theirs is a public trust for which they are publicly responsible.

We need specific goals: 1) *Freedom of speech.* Prior censorship of books and other writings should be stopped. 2) *Freedom of assembly.* The right to associate with others of the same interests should be guaranteed. The right to promulgate minority opinions needs to be protected. 3) *Full participation in the decisions of authority* by all church members—through election of officials, determination of policies at public meetings and hearings, and so on. 4) *Open financial records* of all church revenue and expenditures. 5) *Open personnel files* on all church employees, lay and clerical. 6) *Adequate grievance machinery* to guarantee a fair hearing to all church members. Church employees especially have the right to professional freedom to exercise their ministry in the way they see fit. They must be guaranteed the best possible working situation if they are to be effective. 7) *An independent judiciary* before which canon lawyers can practice law without threat from their bishops or outside interests. 8) *Full submission of the church to secular law.* Exemptions, privileges, and immunities from the law violate the church's mission of promoting the ethical progress of mankind. The church should rather be the first institution to shoulder the responsibilities of institutional citizenship in all countries. The freedom of the church in most societies no longer depends upon a status of privilege and immunity. It can work more effectively within society, if it is a legal part of it. Submission to the constitution as the highest law of the land will be a great boon to the progress of law and democracy. 9) *A constitution of the Roman Church* that will clearly spell out the basic rights and responsibilities of all members.

Essential targets of revolution are:

1. *The privilege of the forum,* which forbids Catholics from taking clerics to court without permission of a bishop or higher authority. Canon 120 of the Code of Canon Law

is the culprit and should be immediately abolished along with Canon 2341, which levies the sanction of automatic excommunication upon offenders. These canons are responsible for making the church legally irresponsible. One should not have to give up any civil rights upon entering the church; rather, he should be supported in the exercise of those rights. In whatever country the church exists, the people agree that the constitution is the highest law of the land and the church should be the first to give due allegiance. It should be open to the legal processes of civil society.

2. *Punishment without due process.* Perhaps the most anachronistic law in the church is Canon 2222, which allows a bishop to punish a cleric without due process or showing cause. He may even suspend clerics from their priestly functions even though it seems only probable that an offense has been committed. These provisions hearken back to the days in England when the star-chamber courts could secretly proceed on mere rumor without examining witnesses, apply torture, and render harsh sentences for a wide variety of cases. In the church today, the bishop is often the employer, plaintiff, prosecutor, judge, jury, and executor of clerical defendants. Although in theory his subjects have the right to appeal to a higher authority, that right is not guaranteed by any legal process. The complaint is often returned for disposition by the *superior against whom it was made!* In effect there is no right to appeal a just grievance within the church. The same principles hold true for the church as for secular society: no one should be deprived of the exercise of his rights *without due process.* Violation of these principles renders the church an outlaw church obstructing the course of justice in a free society.

3. *Ecclesiastical censures.* The sanctions of excommunication, suspension, and interdict come down to us from the time when the church was a separate and perfect society, with its own separate courts and jurisdiction. A person came under either civil law or church law. Now this is not the

case today; civil law is totally competent to regulate the civil conduct of citizens. The church should not interfere with that function without a special reason for intervention. The church no longer needs a penal system of its own to promote the good conduct of its members. Such a system, in fact, is repugnant to its purposes of persuasion and self-determination. As in other voluntary societies, the church can limit its discipline to the good order of the institution by confining punishments to purely administrative, not doctrinal or devotional, affairs. If a Catholic is buried in a non-Catholic cemetery, for example, the church has no need to impose the additional burden of an ecclesiastical penalty for the violation of a church law. Such a practice does not serve to educate people in the voluntariness of the Christian ethic. In our society, Sunday attendance at Mass, Friday abstinence, and the Lenten fast are matters of personal choice. The laws of the church should reflect and support that freedom of choice. All ecclesiastical censures should be abolished. Discipline can be enforced by the dismissal of offenders from their office or from the assembly in which they disturb order and due process.

Some question the ability to reform the church without a bloody revolution. Fortunately, there are new tools available, in and outside the church for the work that has to be done. The first is use of the freedoms and processes available in secular society. The use of the secular press to create pressures for reform and ethical standards within the church has already been successful. The admonition not to wash the dirty linen of the church in public carries little weight in a modern society. If the linen is not washed in public, or if the threat is not there of doing so, it does not get washed at all. One of the basic principles of good government and business management is to keep those in charge on their toes by constant threat of dismissal for reasons of incompetence and failure to inform themselves accurately of situations. The secular communications media provide not only a channel of communication for the people to air their needs but also a means of creating pressures for change. Nothing promotes professional responsibility as well as having to account to the public.

A second tool is the use of the civil courts and legislative system. This always causes some consternation until it is pointed out that they are being effectively used to *prevent* reform in the church. Why cannot they be used instead to further church reform? Fair employment practice laws, for example, often excuse religious institutions from compliance, thereby undermining the responsibilities of the church and the rights of prospective employees. The church's position as a nonprofit and tax-exempt institution makes it responsible in a special way to the general public. Open and public financial statements are demanded by this responsibility. By using the courts to open the records to public view, Catholics will be able to see how their money is being spent and to take some added responsibility for it. Civil rights laws can likewise be used to bring about personnel practices that are based on equity of process instead of expediency.

The civil courts can be used more to introduce and support justice within the church. The courts of land exist to protect due process and the rights of individuals, even when they are violated within private institutions. Traditionally, they do not interfere with the internal workings of government agencies or business unless they are presented with a case by a person with a grievance. Human dignity is sacred in all situations and institutions; it is always wrong to deprive a person of his rights arbitrarily. The courts exist to give the man with little or no protection some means of remedying the wrong, even when no contract has been violated. By making good use of the courts, members of organizations force their organizations into line with accepted principles of equity and fairness.

The courts of our country have been reluctant to act on

cases involving the internal affairs of the church. But there does exist a body of case law in which the courts have acted to determine whether the discipline of the churches themselves have been fairly administered. If a minister brings a suit against his church for arbitrary dismissal, the courts take it upon themselves merely to inquire if the processes set up by the church for such cases were complied with. But what about the Roman Church, in which there are not only no due processes set up for the dismissal of priests from an office, but also a canon law which relieves the church from due process at the discretion of the bishop? The prohibition against priests taking their case to the civil courts hardly remedies the situation. It is likely that if such a dismissal were ever contested in a civil court a decision may be rendered that not only enjoins the reinstatement of the priest, but also requires the church to set up some ethical procedures that would protect church personnel against arbitrary action. I believe that such actions will be needed to impress upon the church the need for higher standards of practice.

Next, there is the need of incorporating into the church the processes of parliamentary procedure and representation that guarantee the right of all to make their voice heard in church policies. Vital communication between the people and their rulers can never be taken for granted, but must be zealously promoted. In some instances, the participation of clerics and lay people in the government of the church has already been arranged. This must expand to include the whole church, from the top to the bottom. In a very real sense, each Christian bears a responsibility for the whole church, sometimes a very urgent responsibility. We never know where the Holy Spirit will speak and act to bring some new insight necessary for the progress of the church. It is necessary to keep the lines of criticism, protest, and accusation open to all. In any organization, success often depends upon the arrangement of a working relationship between the official leadership and the real, prophetical leadership, which can spring up anywhere, in anybody. The formation of parish and diocesan councils made up of representatives from the various interest groups and given legislative power can serve to liberate the prophetical spirit within the church. But the full participation of all members in these democratic processes must be constantly promoted lest they become the entrenched citadels of just another oligarchy. The communications must be kept open between individual members and their immediate representatives; this can only be done by group interaction with them.

The presence of lay people, clerics, and religious on a legislative council would be a graphic representation of what we mean by the term Mystical Body of Christ. The proportion of power given to the bishop, the pastor, assistant priests, nuns, and lay representatives is a constitutional problem demanding political insight. For a beginning, there is good reason to accept one representative from each bona fide group that offers one. Various duties and responsibilities can be assigned to such a council, and others can be assigned to meetings of the general membership.

Such participation of course includes the control of church funds. How the money is controlled is a key issue of church reform. Money talks; the financial structure of the church tells the world more about what it thinks and believes than anything else can. We can preach and preach on human dignity and God's love for man, but as long as the finances of the church remain solely in the hands of clerics, our actions will betray our true convictions. The millions of dollars acquired and spent by the church each week represent the power and dedication of the people *to do something*. It is part of their responsibility to direct that power and serve the interests urged by Christ. It is not their option to relinquish that responsibility to others; men are accountable for the money they give to others, even to the church. A great factor in the development of responsibility and initiative in the laity will be their freedom to participate in that financial responsibility of the church.

A final tool of reform will be the professional organization of priests and religious. Participation and representation by all in the government of the church will satisfy certain needs of the church as a society. But the church is more than a simple society made up of members and officers; it is also a *company* that employs a full-time staff. This situation gives rise to an employer-employee relationship. On the one hand there are the employers: bishops, pastors, chancery officials, superiors of religious orders, and administrators of church institutions. On the other hand there are the employees: assistant pastors, members of religious communities (priests, brothers, or nuns), and lay employees. These are the *professional workers* of the church, to be distinguished from *voluntary church workers* by reason of the source of their income. They work for the church for a living. As much as we would like to avoid casting this situation in such prosaic terms in favor of a more familial relationship governed by mutual trust and love, it is more accurate. The communities in our rectories and convents are not voluntary associations or communities of the spirit, but situations dictated by regulations and administrative decisions. A realistic approach to personnel relationships demands the utilization of the same procedures and insights that have aided in the relationships between business and labor. The policies of American business, in fact, have been adopted wholesale by church administrators—not only business office equipment, but also the business office ethic.

The resulting personnel problems that have developed from this situation for the church in America can be handled with the same tools recommended by the church for secular industries: independent unions and collective bargaining. As shocking as this proposal may sound, usually the objections to it fail to take the realities of the problem into account: priests and nuns quite frequently lack the freedom they need to do their job as they see it should be done. A basic job of reform will be for them to provide for themselves the professional freedom to which they have a right by reason of their vocation.

It has been remarked that the recent discussion and pronouncement concerning the collegiality of the bishops, by which they share with the pope the responsibility for the whole church, is valid only to the extent that they are involved in the pastoral work of the church. But most bishops exercise only part of their pastoral functions, concentrating on administration and leaving the greater burden of teaching to their subordinates, priests, religious, and laymen. It would seem by reason of the arguments presented on the council floor that those who share in the distinctly hierarchical functions of bishops share also their responsibility. This demands a degree of professional freedom necessary to carry out their function. They are not mere flunkies carrying out the orders of superiors, but workers professionally trained to exercise their own initiative and imagination in the tasks they face.

The main task of the church is to persuade people to follow God's law. There are none more directly involved in this task than those dealing directly with people in the pastoral situations of the parish. They know the parish situation and are more familiar than administrators with the problems of people. It is the duty of church administrators, therefore, to place priests, religious, and teachers in the best possible pastoral situation. But this is something only the professional workers in the church can determine. No matter how many years the administrators have spent in the directly pastoral field, no matter how well read or compassionate, they are presently in a different situation, responding to different needs and pressures. Because of the different points of view of the employers and employees in the church, there always arise conflicts of interest. This situation is not only normal; it is good. But there must be a way found to resolve these conflicts. Up until now, the church continued on the supposition that reconciliation was impossible and the problem could be resolved only by vanquishing one side. Many now feel, however, that if the professional workers in the church doubt the wisdom of a superior's policy, they owe it to themselves and to the church to remedy this grievance. Professional organization and collective bargaining give them the means to do this.

The rise of unionism has been one of the great social developments of our century. More than any other movement, it has been responsible for the growth of citizenship and democracy. The growing involvement of the minority groups, students, and teachers in the life of our country is largely the result of the philosophy and techniques of nonviolent protest developed by the unions. Organization and collective bargaining give the individual the power to say no to the power structure and get away with it; they enable him to deal with his employer or superior on an equal and adult basis. Only by structural equity can the inevitable difference of interests be fairly solved.

Objections to the unionization of ministers and priests has been largely based on 1) the denial of an employer-employee relationship within the clergy, 2) the denial that differences of interest really exist between employees and employers, or 3) the need for institutional solidarity among clergy. The first two points have already been touched upon. The third can be answered by suggesting the advantages to be gained by the professional independence of church workers. First of all, just the admission of an employer-employee relationship within the church would go a long way in clarifying the nature of the church. Such a relationship bespeaks of a task, a job to be done in the mutual action and reaction of workers and administrators. The clear demarcation of these two elements in the professional church would make it evident that the church is here *to do something,* not just to collect members and money.

Secondly, by revealing the fact that the professional workers (priests, nuns, and lay employees we are talking about) are really in a working situation, they are brought into contact with the problems of workers in other industries and will be able to relate much better to them. Professional people such as teachers, professors, and social workers were quite surprised, when they formed unions, how much they have in common with trade and industrial workers, how similar is the employee-employer relationship in all areas of life. Even more important, it brought them into the social issues confronting the ordinary workman. The advantages of this type of contact with other employees will greatly offset, for priests, the loss of dubious clerical prestige they now value so highly in their community. Priests and ministers should come to grips with the fact that they are workers employed by an organization for a certain task and that the clerical privileges accorded them by the community are nothing more than the pay-off necessary to keep them from doing their job and possibly stirring up trouble.

Thirdly, and most important, the freedom of the professional church workers would guarantee the freedom of the whole church. The administrators of the church are almost necessarily aligned with the wealthy donors of the community or at least governed largely by their interests. This can hardly be otherwise in an era so committed to grand building programs. The work of the church, especially among the poor and minority groups, thereby suffers greatly owing to the lack of professional freedom in those actually doing the pastoral work of the church. A church worker cannot afford to get too involved because of his lack of protection against the resistance of his bishop, who is committed to support the power structure. Even more, the professional workers cannot become active citizens in the affairs of the community as individuals, thereby robbing their clients of the example of good citizenship. The main reason the laity are so uninvolved in community issues is that their priests, for the most part, are forbidden by political motives from taking part. The church worker, then, is the key man in church reform. Unless he gains freedom to dedicate himself to his task in the manner for which he was trained and to which he aspired, the church's leadership will continue to fail.

The chief objects of the union organization of priests should be 1) a written contract clearly defining the terms of employment, 2) a professional salary, and 3) adequate grievance machinery. The first is the most important. A contract that will hold up in court is the most reliable guarantee of security and freedom necessary for the best professional performance. Such a contract should be temporary and renewable.

A professional salary is also needed for professional freedom. When a priest must rely upon the monthly allowance of one hundred dollars or so, he does not dare to challenge his relationship with his employer. This, I believe, is one of the most important reasons church workers relinquish their responsibilities in a time of crisis; they just cannot financially afford to buck the decisions of their superiors. Even more important, a professional salary (three thousand dollars yearly plus room and board) will relieve the clergy of the burden of relying upon the patronage of the wealthy. The whole system of stole fees, Mass stipends, and special collections for the clergy works to align them with the rich. When priests are dependent upon such means, they naturally gravitate toward the wealthier parishes. It is imperative for the church that priests be publicly accountable for every penny of income. Professional salaries would go a long way in accomplishing this.

Democratic structures and unions may appear as solutions that are too human for the church. But it is the human church that we are dealing with. Human problems demand human answers. If the answers to the church's problems do not come from man, they will not come at all. God has shown his hand; he is fully committed to the human way of doing things.

A SELECT BOOKLIST

SECTION ONE: THE THEOLOGY OF REFORM

Bentham, Jeremy. *The Handbook of Political Fallacies.* Harper Torchbooks. New York: Harper & Brothers, 1962.

Bentham, Jeremy, and Mill, John Stuart. *The Utilitarians,* an *Introduction to the Principles of Morals and Legislation, Utilitarianism, and On Liberty.* Dolphin Books. Garden City: Doubleday & Company, Inc., 1961.

Berger, Peter L. *The Noise of the Solemn Assemblies: Christian Commitment and the Religious Establishment in America.* Garden City: Doubleday & Company, Inc., 1961.

Bray, Allen F., III. *The Return to Self-concern.* Philadelphia: The Westminster Press, 1964.

Brewster, R. Wallace. *Government in Modern Society, With Emphasis on American Institutions.* Boston: Houghton Mifflin Company, 1958.

Buber, Martin. *Between Man and Man.* Boston: Beacon Press, 1955.

——. *I and Thou.* Second Edition. New York: Charles Scribner's Sons, 1958.

——. *The Prophetic Faith.* New York: Harper & Brothers, 1960.

Callahan, Daniel J. *Honesty in the Church.* New York: Charles Scribner's Sons, 1965.

Callahan, Daniel J.; Oberman, Heiko A.; and O'Hanlon, Daniel J., S.J., eds. *Christianity Divided.* New York: Sheed & Ward, 1961.

Campbell, Will D. *Race and the Renewal of the Church.* Philadelphia: The Westminster Press, 1962.

Carter, Gwendolen M., and Herz, John H. *Government and Politics in the Twentieth Century.* New York: Frederick A. Praeger, Inc., 1961.

Congar, Yves, O.P. *Power and Poverty in the Church.* Baltimore: Helicon Press, Inc., 1964.

Cox, Harvey. *The Secular City: Secularization and Urbanization in the Theological Perspective.* New York: The Macmillan Company, 1965.

de Raeymaeker Louis, *et al. Truth and Freedom.* Pittsburgh: Duquesne University Press, 1955.

Fesquet, Henri. *Catholicism: Religion of Tomorrow?* New York: Holt, Rinehart and Winston, Inc., 1964.

Fields, Guy. *Political Theory.* New York: A. S. Barnes & Co., Inc., 1957.

Friedrich, Carl J., ed. *Authority.* New York: Liberal Arts Press, 1958.

———. *Constitutional Government and Democracy.* Revised Edition. Boston: Blaisdell Publishing Co., 1950.

———. ed. *Totalitarianism.* The Universal Library. New York: Grosset & Dunlap, Inc., 1964.

Häring, Bernard, C.SS.R. *The Law of Christ.* 3 vols. Westminster, Md.: The Newman Press, 1961.

Herberg, Will. *Protestant-Catholic-Jew: An Essay in American Religious Sociology.* A New Edition. Anchor Books. Garden City: Doubleday & Company, Inc., 1955.

Howe, Reuel L. *Man's Need and God's Action.* Greenwich, Conn.: The Seabury Press, Inc., 1953.

Jefferson, P. C., ed. *The Church in the 60's.* Greenwich, Conn.: The Seabury Press, Inc., 1962.

Kean, Charles D. *The Christian Gospel and the Parish Church.* Greenwich, Conn.: The Seabury Press, Inc., 1953.

Küng, Hans. *The Council, Reform, and Reunion.* New York: Sheed & Ward, 1961.

Lenski, Gerhard. *The Religious Factor, A Sociological Study of Religion's Impact on Politics, Economics, and Family Life.* Revised Edition. Anchor Books. Garden City: Doubleday & Company, Inc., 1963.

Lippmann, Walter. *The Public Philosophy.* A Mentor Book. New York: The New American Library of World Literature, Inc., 1956.

Marty, Martin E. *Varieties of Unbelief.* New York: Holt, Rinehart and Winston, Inc., 1964.

Mill, John Stuart. *Utilitarianism, on Liberty, Essay on Bentham.* Meridian Books. Cleveland: The World Publishing Company, 1962.

Mirgeler, Arthur. *Mutations of Western Christianity.* New York: Herder and Herder, Inc., 1964.
Mouroux, Jean. *The Christian Experience.* New York: Sheed & Ward, 1954.
Paine, Thomas. *The Rights of Man.* Everyman's Library. New York: E. P. Dutton & Co., Inc., 1935.
Robinson, John A. T. *Honest to God.* Philadelphia: The Westminster Press, 1963.
Routley, Erik. *The Man for Others.* New York: Oxford University Press, Inc., 1964.
Shinn, Roger L. *Tangled World.* New York: Charles Scribner's Sons, 1965.
Stewart, Michael. *Modern Forms of Government.* New York: Frederick A. Praeger, Inc., 1961.
Stringfellow, William. *Free in Obedience.* New York: The Seabury Press, Inc., 1964.
Suenens, Leon Joseph Cardinal. *The Nun in the World.* Westminster, Md.: The Newman Press, 1962.
Teilhard de Chardin, Pierre. *The Divine Milieu.* New York: Harper & Brothers, 1960.
——. *The Phenomenon of Man.* Harper Torchbooks. New York: Harper & Brothers, 1959.
Trueblood, Elton. *The Company of the Committed.* New York: Harper & Row, Publishers, 1961.
Washington, Joseph R., Jr. *Black Religion, The Negro and Christianity in the United States.* Boston: Beacon Press, 1964.
Winter, Gibson. *The New Creation as Metropolis.* New York: The Macmillan Company, 1963.
——. *The Suburban Captivity of the Churches.* New York: The Macmillan Company, 1962.

SECTION TWO: THE SECULAR CONCERNS OF THE CHURCH

Abell, Aaron I. *American Catholicism and Social Action: a Search for Social Justice, 1865–1950.* Garden City: Hanover House, 1960.
Allport, Gordon. *The Nature of Prejudice.* New York: Doubleday & Company, Inc., 1958.

Arendt, Hannah. *The Human Condition.* Anchor Books. New York: Doubleday & Company, Inc., 1959.

Baldwin, James. *The Fire Next Time.* New York: The Dial Press, Inc., 1963.

Bardolph, Richard. *The Negro Vanguard.* Vintage Books. New York: Random House, Inc., 1961.

Barnes, Roswell P. *Under Orders: The Churches and Public Affairs.* Garden City: Doubleday & Company, Inc., 1961.

Conant, James B. *Slums and Suburbs.* A Signet Book. New York: The New American Library of World Literature, Inc., 1961.

Douglas, Dr. Mary, *et al.*, eds. *Man in Society: Patterns of Human Organization.* Doubleday Pictorial Library. Garden City: Doubleday & Company, Inc., 1964.

DuBois, W. E. Burghardt. *The Souls of Black Folk.* Crest Book. Greenwich, Conn.: Fawcett Publications, Inc., 1961.

Dunne, George H., ed. *Poverty in Plenty.* New York: P. J. Kenedy & Sons, 1964.

Galbraith, John Kenneth. *The Affluent Society.* A Mentor Book. New York: The New American Library of World Literature, Inc., 1958.

Ginzberg, Eli, ed. *Values and Ideals of American Youth.* New York: Columbia University Press, 1961.

Griffin, John Howard. *Black Like Me.* A Signet Book. New York: The New American Library of World Literature, Inc., 1961.

Harrington, Michael. *The Other America.* New York: The Macmillan Company, 1962.

Hughes, Langston. *Fight for Freedom: the Story of the NAACP.* New York: Berkley Publishing Corporation, 1962.

John XXIII, Pope. *Mater et Magistra, Christianity and Social Progress.* New York: The America Press, 1961.

——. *Pacem in Terris.* New York: The America Press, 1962.

Keith-Lucas, Alan. *The Church and Social Welfare.* Philadelphia: The Westminster Press, 1962.

Keys, Donald, ed. *God and the H-bomb.* New York: Bellmeadows Press, 1961.

King, Martin Luther. *Why We Can't Wait.* New York: Harper & Row, Publishers, 1963.

Krech, David, *et al.* *The Individual in Society.* New York: McGraw-Hill Book Company, 1962.

National Council of Churches, Department of Migrant Work. *Let Justice Roll Down, Ethical Issues in the Relations between Growers and Seasonal Workers in Industrialized Agriculture.* New York: National Council of the Churches of Christ in the U.S.A., 1963.

Packard, Vance. *Status Seekers.* New York: David McKay Co., Inc., 1959.

Pierre, Abbé. *Man Is Your Brother.* Westminster, Md.: The Newman Press, 1958.

President's Committee on Youth Employment. *The Challenge of Jobless Youth.* Washington: U. S. Dept. of Labor, 1963.

Raab, Earl, and Folk, Hugh. *The Pattern of Dependent Poverty in California.* Sacramento: Welfare Study Commission, 1963.

Riesman, David. *The Lonely Crowd.* New Haven: Yale University Press, 1961.

Rowland, Stanley J., Jr. *Ethics, Crime, and Redemption.* Philadelphia: The Westminster Press, 1963.

Schindler-Rainman, Eva. *A Unique New Venture, South Central Volunteer Bureau Los Angeles.* Los Angeles: South Central Volunteer Bureau, 1965.

Seifert, Harvey. *Ethical Resources for International Relations.* Philadelphia: The Westminster Press, 1964.

Silberman, Charles E. *Crisis in Black and White.* New York: Random House, Inc., 1964.

Stringfellow, William. *My People Is the Enemy.* New York: Holt, Rinehart and Winston, Inc., 1964.

Woodward, C. Vann. *The Strange Career of Jim Crow.* A Galaxy Book. New York: Oxford University Press, Inc., 1957.

Wright, Richard. *White Man, Listen!* Anchor Books. Garden City: Doubleday & Company, Inc., 1964.

SECTION THREE: RELIGIOUS EDUCATION

Allport, Gordon. *Becoming.* New Haven: Yale University Press, 1955.

Bayne, Stephen F. *Christian Living.* Greenwich, Conn.: The Seabury Press, Inc., 1957.

Bergevin, Paul, and McKinley, John. *Design for Adult Education in the Church.* Greenwich, Conn.: The Seabury Press, Inc., 1958.

Bergevin, Paul; Morris, Dwight; and Smith, Robert M. *Adult Education Procedures.* Greenwich, Conn.: The Seabury Press, Inc., 1963.

Boehlke, Robert R. *Theories of Learning in Christian Education.* Philadelphia: The Westminster Press, 1962.

Cully, Iris V. *Imparting the Word: The Bible in Christian Education.* Philadelphia: The Westminster Press, 1962.

——. *The Dynamics of Christian Education.* Philadelphia: The Westminster Press, 1958.

Forell, George W. *Ethics of Decision.* Philadelphia: The Muhlenberg Press, 1955.

Gilbert, W. Kent. *As Christians Teach.* Philadelphia: Lutheran Church Press, 1962.

Gordon, Thomas. *Group-centered Leadership.* New York: Houghton Mifflin Company, 1955.

Hare, A. Paul; Borgatta, Edgar F.; and Bales, Robert F. *Small Groups.* New York: Alfred A. Knopf, Inc., 1955.

Heikkinen, Jacob, and Norquist, N. Leroy. *Helping Youth and Adults Know the Bible.* Philadelphia: Lutheran Church Press, 1962.

Herzel, Catherine. *Helping Children Worship.* Philadelphia: Lutheran Church Press, 1963.

Hofinger, Johannes, S.J., ed. *Teaching All Nations: a Symposium on Modern Catechetics.* New York: Herder and Herder, Inc., 1961.

Howe, Reuel L. *The Creative Years.* Greenwich, Conn.: The Seabury Press, Inc., 1959.

Hunter, David. *Christian Education as Engagement.* Greenwich, Conn.: The Seabury Press, Inc., 1963.

Jungmann, Josef A. *Handing On the Faith.* New York: Herder and Herder, Inc., 1959.

Kaufman, Gordon. *The Context of Decision.* New York: Abingdon Press, 1961.

Lasker, Bruno. *Democracy Through Discussion.* New York: H. W. Wilson Co., 1949.

Lazareth, William H., and Garhart, Majorie F. *Helping Children Know Doctrine.* Philadelphia: Lutheran Church Press, 1962.

Lewis, Eve. *Children and Their Religion.* New York: Sheed & Ward, 1962.

Lifton, Walter M. *Working with Groups.* New York: John Wiley & Sons, Inc., 1961.

Lutheran Boards of Education. *The Age Group Objectives of Christian Education.* (Prepared in connection with the Long-Range Program of Lutheran Boards of Parish Education.) Philadelphia: United Lutheran Churches of America, 1958.

Miller, Randolph C. *Biblical Theology and Christian Education.* New York: Charles Scribner's Sons, 1956.

——. *Christian Nurture and the Church.* New York: Charles Scribner's Sons, 1961.

——. *Education for Christian Living.* Englewood Cliffs, N.J.: Prentice-Hall, Inc., 1963.

Montagu, M. F. Ashley. *On Being Human.* New York: Henry Schuman, Inc., Publishers, 1950.

Oraison, Marc. *Love or Constraint?* Deus Books. New York: Paulist Press, 1961.

Robinson, James H., *et al. Education for Decision.* New York: The Seabury Press, Inc., 1963.

Ryan, Mary Perkins. *Are Parochial Schools the Answer?* New York: Holt, Rinehart and Winston, Inc., 1964.

Sherrill, Lewis J. *The Gift of Power.* New York: The Macmillan Company, 1956.

Sloyan, Gerard S. *Modern Catechetics.* New York: The Macmillan Company, 1963.

Sloyan, Gerard S., *et al. Shaping the Christian Message.* Deus Books. Glen Rock, N.J.: Paulist Press, 1963.

Standing, E. M. *Maria Montessori, Her Life and Work.* A Mentor-Omega Book. New York: The New American Library of World Literature, Inc., 1962.

Straus, Bert and Frances. *New Ways to Better Meetings.* New York: The Viking Press, Inc., 1964.

Swift, Henry and Elizabeth. *Community Groups and You.* New York: The John Day Company, 1964.

U. S. Department of Labor. *Design for Community Action.* Washington: U. S. Government Printing Office, 1962.

SECTION FOUR: BIBLE READING AIDS

Albright, William Foxwell. *From the Stone Age to Christianity.* Second Edition. Anchor Books. Garden City: Doubleday & Company, Inc., 1957.

Bruns, J. Edgar. *Hear His Voice Today, A Guide to the Content and Comprehension of the Bible.* New York: P. J. Kenedy & Sons, 1963.

Charlier, Dom Celestin. *The Christian Approach to the Bible.* Westminster, Md.: The Newman Press, 1958.

Daniel-Rops, Henri. *Jesus and His Times.* 2 vols. Image Books. Garden City: Doubleday & Company, Inc., 1958.

——. *Daily Life in the Time of Jesus.* New York: Hawthorn Books, Inc., 1962.

Dannemiller, Lawrence, S.S. *Reading the Word of God.* Baltimore: Helicon Press, Inc., 1960.

deDietrich Suzanne. *God's Unfolding Purpose, A Guide to the Study of the Bible.* Philadelphia: The Westminster Press, 1960.

——. *The Witnessing Community, The Biblical Record of God's Purpose.* Philadelphia: The Westminster Press, 1958.

Denton, Robert C. *The Holy Scriptures–A Survey.* Greenwich, Conn.: The Seabury Press, Inc., 1960.

Jones, Alexander. *God's Living Word.* New York: Sheed & Ward, 1961.

Miller, Madeleine S., and Lane, J. *Harper's Bible Dictionary.* 7th ed. Harper & Brothers, 1961.

Newland, Mary Reed. *The Family and the Bible.* New York: Random House, Inc., 1963.

Poelman, Abbe Roger. *How to Read the Bible.* New York: P. J. Kenedy & Sons, 1953.

Richardson, Alan, ed. *A Theological Wordbook of the Bible.* New York: The Macmillan Company, 1950.

Staack, Hagen. *Living Personalities of the Old Testament.* New York: Harper & Row, Publishers, 1964.

Weiser, Artur. *The Psalms.* Philadelphia: The Westminster Press, 1962.

Wright, G. Ernest, and Fuller, Reginald H. *The Book of the Acts of God.* Anchor Books. New York: Doubleday & Company, Inc., 1960.

SECTION FIVE: CHRISTIAN WORSHIP RESOURCES

Abba, Raymond. *Principles of Christian Worship with Special References to the Free Churches.* New York: Oxford University Press, Inc., 1960.

Bailey, Albert E. *The Gospel in Hymns.* New York: Charles Scribner's Sons, 1950.

Book of Common Prayer. Copies of the U.S. 1928, the Canadian 1959, the Scottish 1929, the English 1662 and the 1928 Proposed, and the other forms of the Prayer Book can be obtained from Oxford University Press, Inc., or Cambridge University Press.

Braso, Gabriel M. *Liturgy and Spirituality.* Collegeville, Minn.: The Liturgical Press, 1960.

Delling, Gerhard. *Worship in the New Testament.* Philadelphia: The Westminster Press, 1962.

Dix, Dom Gregory. *The Shape of the Liturgy.* Naperville, Ill.: Alec R. Allenson, Inc., 1960.

Freer, Harold Wiley, and Hall, Francis B. *Two or Three Together, A Manual for Prayer Groups.* New York: Harper & Row, Publishers, 1954.

Harton, Sibyl. *To Make Intercession.* New York: Morehouse-Barlow Co., Inc., 1964.

Jones, B. H. *The American Lectionary.* New York: Morehouse-Gorham Company, 1944.

Jungmann, Josef A. *The Early Liturgy, To the Time of Gregory the Great.* Notre Dame, Ind.: Notre Dame University Press, 1959.

——. *The Eucharistic Prayer.* Notre Dame, Ind.: Fides Publishers, Inc., 1960.

——. *The Mass of the Roman Rite, Its Origins and Development (Missarum Sollemnia).* New revised and abridged edition in one volume. New York: Benziger Brothers, Inc., 1959.

Kuhn, Roger P. *The Mass Reformed, A New Draft Reshaping Public Worship for Relevance Today.* Notre Dame, Ind.: The Catholic Action Press, 1965.

Lutheran Churches Cooperating in the Commission on the Liturgy and Hymnal. *Service Book and Hymnal,* 1958.

The Methodist Church. *The Book of Worship for Church and Home.* Nashville: The Methodist Publishing House, 1965.

Morsch, Vivian Sharp. *The Use of Music in Christian Education.* Philadelphia: The Westminster Press, 1956.

Nocent, Adrien. *The Future of the Liturgy.* New York: Herder and Herder, Inc., 1963.

The (United) Presbyterian Church in the USA, the Joint Committee on Worship. *Service for the Lord's Day and Lectionary for the Christian Year.* Philadelphia: The Westminster Press, 1964.

Price, Carl F. *One Hundred and one Hymn Stories.* New York: Abingdon Press, 1951.

Protestant Episcopal Church in the USA. *The Hymnal 1940.* New York: The Church Pension Fund, 1943.

——. *The Hymnal 1940 Companion.* Third Revised Edition. New York: The Church Pension Fund, 1951.

Protestant Episcopal Church in the USA, The Standing Liturgical Commission of. *Prayer Book Studies.* 12-part paperback. New York: The Church Pension Fund, 1953.

Robinson, John A. T. *Liturgy Coming to Life.* London: R. A. Mowbray & Company, Limited. 1963.

Routley, Eric. *Church Music and Theology.* Philadelphia: The Muhlenberg Press, 1959.

Shepherd, Massey H., Jr. *The Oxford American Prayer Book Commentary.* New York: Oxford University Press, Inc., 1950.

——. *The Worship of the Church.* Greenwich, Conn.: The Seabury Press, Inc., 1952.

Vagaggini, Cyprian, O.S.B. *Theological Dimensions of the Liturgy.* Collegeville, Minn.: The Liturgical Press, 1959.

Wigan, Bernard, ed. *The Liturgy in English.* London: Oxford University Press, Inc., 1962.

Williams, John G. *Worship and the Modern Child.* New York: The Macmillan Company, 1958.